The Word Whiz's Guide to

New York Middle School Vocabulary

By Chris Kensler

A Paper Airplane Project

Simon & Schuster
New York ● London ● Sydney ● Singapore ● Toronto

Kaplan Publishing
Published by Simon & Schuster, Inc.
1230 Avenue of the Americas
New York, NY 10020

For bulk sales to schools, colleges, and universities, please contact: Order Department, Simon & Schuster, 100
Front Street, Riverside, NJ 08075. Phone: 1-800-223-2336. Fax: 1-800-943-9831.

Kaplan® is a registered trademark of Kaplan, Inc.

Cover Design: Cheung Tai
Interior Page Design and Production: Paper Airplane Projects

Manufactured in the United States of America

September 2001

10 9 8 7 6 5 4 3 2 1

Library of Congress Cataloging-in-Publication Data

ISBN 0-7432-1105-7

All of the practice questions in this book were created by the authors to illustrate question types. They are not
actual test questions.

Table of Contents

About the Author

Chris Kensler grew up in Indiana and attended Indiana University, where he majored in English. He has edited test prep publications, worked as feature writer/reporter for a daytime drama publication, and written a few books, including *Study Smart Junior*, which received the Parents' Choice Award. Currently, he is the editor of an art magazine, is married to the lovely woman who designed this book, and has some cool cats and a dog named Joe.

Stan Hattan is a figment of his imagination.

Acknowledgments

The author would like to thank Maureen McMahon, Lori DeGeorge, and Beth Grupper for their help in shaping and editing the manuscript, and Chris Dreyer for copyediting this book.

The publisher wishes to thank Karen Daley for her contributions to this book.

Introduction

Hi. My name is Stan. Stan Hattan. As you can

probably guess from my name, I live in New York, New York: the town so nice they named it twice. I'm going to help you with your vocabulary.

I'm in the eighth grade. At my school I'm famous for two things—my fastball and my vocabulary. I perfected my fastball last summer by throwing at a 2 foot x 2 foot box on a diamond in Central Park every morning. Man, my arm felt like a rubber band at first, but now it is strong and my fastball is up to 60 mph—not bad for an eighth grader.

I perfected my vocabulary by practicing, too. By reading books, writing essays and stories, and by just generally paying attention to words. It turned me into a Word Whiz. Now I'm going to turn you into one.

If you're having trouble on tests, one reason might be because you are having trouble understanding the words. Of course, the first and most likely reason you blank or panic or freak out on tests is that instead of studying, you keep watching your new *Chicken Run* DVD. (Believe me, I don't hold it against you, that flick rocks.) Still, sometimes things don't go so well even when you do study. That's the worst. You're like—I studied all night and I still got a D! What's up with that?

Sometimes it's because you just aren't comfortable with the words on the test. For example, say you are taking a math test and one of the questions asks you to find the "perimeter of a rectangle." It's not hard to do—you just add up all the sides. But if you space out on what the word "perimeter" means, you're in trouble. Your brain freezes. Does it have something to do with periscopes? Or maybe something to do with meters? The next thing you know, you have a picture of a submarine doing the 40-meter dash in your head.

Believe me, I've been there. It's no fun. But it doesn't have to be that way.

Word Whiz Is Here to Help

Believe it or not, you probably already know more than 10,000 words total. It just happens. The older you get, the more words get added to your vocabulary. But let's not talk about the words you already know, let's focus on the words you need to know. The 600-plus words in this book are the most important ones to know for middle school homework, exams, and the New York State tests. I call them WhizWords. If you know these WhizWords backward and forward, you will be in good shape at school, and you will no doubt become rich and successful when you grow up.

I'm going to review these WhizWords for you by relating them to things you're probably interested in, like TV, movies, sports, music, celebrities, and the stuff kids like us like to do when we're NOT in school. All these things can help you learn these 600-plus words.

I'm also going to explain them to you in words you already know. The problem with a lot of dictionaries is the words they use in the definition are harder than the word they are defining! Or they just repeat the word. Here's an example—the definition of "impartial" from a popular dictionary (I won't name names):

impartial—*adj.* not partial; unprejudiced.

Gee, thanks a lot! Believe me, if I knew what "partial" meant, I could probably figure out impartial. And "unprejudiced?" How many syllables is that? Eleven? Geez. And of course they don't give a sample sentence. Now here's my definition:

impartial—*adj.* fair. Judges and juries are supposed to be <u>impartial</u>. That means they just go by the facts. Like Judge Judy on TV —she is an <u>impartial</u> judge who listens to all the facts, then she reams the person who is guilty.

Better, right? I'm also only going to give you the one or two meanings that you are most likely to see on a test or in class. Some words have tons of different meanings, and regular dictionaries have to list them all. But in my book, I am just going to focus on the meanings that apply to your tests, classroom reading, and homework.

How to Use This Book

Most dictionaries just list all words in alphabetical order. That's a good idea of course. But I have gone one step further. My WhizWords are divided into six categories:

English Language Arts   **Science**
Social Studies   **Test Instructions**
Math   **All-Purpose Words**

This way, you can focus on the subjects where you want to improve your vocabulary. I've also included a list of words that appear in the instructions on the New York State tests, and another list of "all-purpose" words.

Each of these chapters has two parts—1) the vocabulary list, and 2) some practice exercises. The exercises will help you remember important words that are related to each other. Off to the side of the exercises, you'll see a bunch of icons. These tell you what resources you'll use for the exercise—things like TV, newspapers, and the Internet. These are the icons:

Life   School   Movie   Sports   Magazine

History   Imagination   News   Internet   Television

Think of these exercises as dessert. The main course of the book is my WhizWord lists. They give you easy-to-understand definitions and sample sentences like the one I gave you for "impartial." You'll also find all this extra cool stuff:

 My helpful hints on how to learn words and ace tests.

 *Really* short quizzes to help cement the words in your brain.

 Good stuff to know that is related to a WhizWord.

DOUBLE MEANING WhizWords that can mean two different things.

 Words that mean the same thing as a WhizWord.

 Words that mean the opposite of a WhizWord.

 An important word related to a WhizWord.

 How WhizWords are likely to appear on the New York State tests.

Okay then. I think I'm done explaining. Have fun, and remember, if you learn all these words, your vocabulary will be really, really good and you should do better on your tests. It's a better way to live. Peace.

Stan Hattan

Chapter 1
English Language Arts

Use an adjective or adverb to describe each of these words:
school
shopping
tests
green
sports
chewy

Use the analogy of a staircase to describe how your grades have been going recently:

_____
_____
_____
_____

Related Word

analysis—n.
close study.

adjective—*n*. a word that describes a noun or a pronoun. You need to be able to pick out <u>adjectives</u> in sentences, and you also need to use them when you do your own writing. *Bad, good, stupid, smart, rich,* and *poor* are all <u>adjectives</u>.

adverb—*n*. a word that describes a verb, an adjective, or another adverb. What I just said for adjectives goes for <u>adverbs</u>. You can remember what words an <u>adverb</u> modifies because the parts of speech it modifies are part of its name: ad- (adjectives, adverbs) and -<u>verb</u> (verbs). *Very, really, not, incredibly, amazingly* and *obviously* are all <u>adverbs</u>.

allegory—*n*. a literary device in which the people, places, and things in the story represent moral or religious principles. For example, I am writing a story where I have a slow, dimwitted character with clawlike fingers named Slothy S. Slothster. He represents, you guessed it, a sloth!

alliteration—*n*. the appearance of two or more words with the same initial sound in a sentence or phrase. *Example*: *S*lothy *S*. *S*lothster *s*ank *s*lowly into the *s*ofa, *s*ighing.

analogy—*n*. a comparison between two things, made in order to explain or clarify an idea. *Example*: Red Sox fans and Yankee fans eye each other uneasily in the stands before a big game. Oil and water do not mix.

analyze—*v*. to study carefully to figure out something. I must say, after <u>analyzing</u> all the latest Internet search engines, I still like Yahoo! the best. It is fast, gets me the best results, and is easiest to navigate.

antecedent—*n*. the word or phrase to which a relative pronoun refers. *Example*: Even though *Bernie Williams* broke *his* bat, he still managed to hit the ball out of the park. (*Bernie Williams* is the <u>antecedent</u> to which *his* refers.)

antonym—*n*. the opposite word. *Good* is the <u>antonym</u> of *bad*. *Over* is the <u>antonym</u> of *under*. I have listed <u>antonyms</u> for lots of words throughout this book.

chronological—*adj*. in the order events happened. Tests are always asking you to put events in <u>chronological</u> order, or to be able to take a set of <u>chronological</u> events and write a story about them. Jim Carrey's best movies, in <u>chronological</u> order, are *Ace Ventura: Pet Detective* (1994), *Ace Ventura: When Nature Calls* (1995), *Liar Liar* (1997), and *How the Grinch Stole Christmas* (2000).

clarify—*v.* to make clearer. On tests, you will often be asked to <u>clarify</u> sentences and what characters in stories are talking about. *Example*: "Jim Carrey's comedic brilliance over the span of his film career is unsurpassed in the history of cinema" can be <u>clarified</u> as "Jim Carrey is funnier than anyone, ever."

cliché—*n.* a saying that is used too much. *Example*: It is a <u>cliché</u> to call cafeteria food dog food, because so many people have called it dog food before. In general, when writing a story, you want to avoid using <u>clichés</u>.

climax—*n.* the big event that a story builds toward. Stories of suspense usually have the biggest, best <u>climaxes</u> because the whole point of a suspense story is to get you on the edge of your seat and then have a big bang at the end.

coherent—*adj.* making sense. It is important that sentences and paragraphs have a <u>coherent</u> structure. If you are telling a story, the first thing comes first, the second thing comes second, and so on. It is also important for people to be <u>coherent</u>. Newscasters, for instance, have to be <u>coherent</u> so we can understand what they're saying.

Antonym
incoherent—**adj.**
confusing.

colloquialism—*n.* a piece of informal speech. I was in England last year and the family I was staying with asked if I liked "bangers and mash." Apparently, that's a <u>colloquialism</u> for sausages served with boiled-then-mashed potatoes. I said "yes" to be polite, but they were just awful.

compare—*v.* to find the similarities. (See *contrast* for more.)

complex—*adj.* complicated, made up of a bunch of connected parts. On lots of tests you are asked to read <u>complex</u> passages and find the important information in them. It's like watching a murder mystery on TV and trying to figure out who did it. The mystery is <u>complex</u>, but if you pay attention and concentrate,

Antonym
simple—**adj.**
easy.

you can figure out who the culprit is.

compound—*adj.* in English Language Arts, a word made of two or more other words is a compound word. *Carpetbagger* (carpet + bagger) is a compound word. (See Social Studies for the definition of *carpetbagger*.) Compound sentences are two sentences connected with a conjunction or a conjunction with a comma. *Example*: I really like her, but I am afraid to talk to her.

concise—*adj.* short and to the point. When you are writing, try to be concise. Judge Judy on TV is very concise in her rulings. She usually says something like "You're wrong, you're an idiot, you're guilty!" Now that's concise.

On the Test

Based on the information given, what conclusion could you arrive at?

conclusion—*n.* judgment or decision. Many tests ask you what conclusion you can draw from a passage or what conclusion someone in a story came to. That just means you need to be able to sum up what you read. *Example*: After I read the box score from the last Yankees game, I came to the conclusion that they need a few more good hitters. Only three guys on the team are hitting over .300.

conflict—*n.* a clash of ideas; a clash of characters. Most interesting stories center around conflict—two people who can't stand each other, or two ideas that are really different. *Example*: I am writing a screenplay called *Pretty Dumb* about two actresses who can't stand each other. There is a lot of conflict between the two.

context—*n.* the setting a word or statement appears in. It's important to know context when you are trying to figure out what someone means. If someone yells "Stop!" the context of that yell tells you why she is yelling. Is her car being stolen? Or is she going to drive off a cliff? If you know the context, you'll understand what is meant.

contrast—*v.* to find the differences. This word is most often used in test questions that ask you to "compare and contrast." That just means write about the similarities and the differences. *Example*: Compare and contrast supermodel/actress James King and actress/pin-up star Pamela Anderson.

WhizTip

To remember credible means "believable," think of incredible, which means "really hard to believe."

credible—*adj.* believable. In a trial, a credible witness is a witness the jury can believe. On a test, a credible answer is one that you think could be true. So if I said Pamela Anderson and James King were both the best actresses in the world, that's not really a credible statement. If I said both are blonde and beautiful—that's credible.

culture—*n.* all of the artistic, scientific, and social accomplishments of a group of people. Basically everything a group of people does makes up that society's culture. Traditionally, American culture has been summed up as "baseball, hot dogs, and apple pie." I'll agree with the baseball part, but I'm not sure about the other two.

dialect—*n.* how a particular part of a country speaks. Where you come from is usually where you get your <u>dialect</u>. There is a soft Southern <u>dialect</u>, the twangy Texas <u>dialect</u>—and of course our famous abrasive Noo Yawk <u>dialect</u>! Authors use <u>dialect</u> in stories to give readers information about character and setting.

euphemism—*n.* the act of substituting an inoffensive word or phrase for an offensive one. For example, "passed away" is a <u>euphemism</u> for "died." "We are in a rebuilding year" is a euphemism in sports for "We are terrible this year, please be patient."

evaluate—*v.* to consider. Tests ask you to <u>evaluate</u> information all of the time. That just means you need to read everything they give you and consider the information before making a decision on an answer. My mom often <u>evaluates</u> the food she is buying at the grocery store by looking at the ingredients to see how much fat is in it. She hates fat.

explicit—*adj.* clearly defined; obvious. My mom got really mad at me yesterday because, last week, she and dad left me alone for the evening with <u>explicit</u> instructions not to call this girl I met at camp long distance. Mom just got the phone bill. Now I'm grounded.

exposition—*n.* a detailed description or explanation of a subject. If you are asked to write an <u>expository</u> essay, your teacher wants you to explain or describe a subject in detail. That's <u>exposition</u>.

fallacy—*n.* a false notion; something that's not true. It is a <u>fallacy</u> to assume that, just because the Yankees keep winning the World Series, they are unbeatable in the playoffs.

figurative language—*n.* the use of metaphors. Instead of writing "Kerry Collins is a great football player," a sports reporter using <u>figurative language</u> would write "Kerry Collins is a football player as great as the Rocky Mountains are tall." (See the definition for *metaphor* for more on this.)

flashback—*n.* a point in a story where the narrative goes back in time for a little while before continuing forward. Books and movies use <u>flashbacks</u> all the time, usually to give you more information about a character or the plot. Sometimes in movies and on TV, they signal a <u>flashback</u> by making the screen get all wiggly or fuzzy.

foreshadow—*v.* to hint at what is to come later in a story. A writer may <u>foreshadow</u> that two young characters are going to get married later in the book by having each of them, separately, talk to people about how much they want to get married when they get older.

genre—*n.* a type of writing. Romance, horror, mystery, and sci-

Whiz Quiz

List three euphemisms you or members of your family use:

1._____
_____

2._____
_____

3._____
_____

Whiz Tip

Remember **flashback** by thinking of the word "back."

Whiz Tip

Remember **foreshadow** by thinking of the word "forward."

fi are all fiction <u>genres</u>. My favorite <u>genre</u> is horror, especially R. L. Stine horror.

homonym—*n.* one of two words that are spelled alike and sound alike but mean different things. *Lie* (to tell an untruth) and *lie* (to rest) are <u>homonyms.</u>

hypothesis—*n.* a proposed explanation for something that happened. I have a <u>hypothesis</u> for why the Giants lost to the Ravens in the Super Bowl in 2001: They were wearing the wrong shoes and couldn't get any traction.

identify—*v.* to pick out. English tests often ask you to <u>identify</u> the protagonist or to <u>identify</u> the verb or to <u>identify</u> the simile.

idiom—*n.* word or phrase that means something it doesn't really mean. Confused? Here are a few <u>idioms</u>:

- *ants in your pants* means *you are fidgety*
- *born with a silver spoon in your mouth* means *your parents are rich*
- *stop bugging me* means *stop bothering me*

imagery—*n.* mental pictures; the use of figurative language to create scenes and moods. Writers use <u>imagery</u> to make their stories more interesting. Here's an example from my screenplay, with the imagery underlined: Pamela Anderson rose from bed and <u>stretched like a baby bird breaking from its egg</u>. She had a hard day ahead. She and James King were up for the same part in the new Jim Carrey movie. Whoever got the part would be the toast of the town. Whoever lost would feel <u>lower than the dirt on the soles of a pair of six-inch stiletto heels</u>. The movie's director, Fabio, held their fates in his hands.

interview—*n.* a conversation in which one person asks the questions and the other answers. One great way to learn about lots of different people is to read <u>interviews</u> with them in magazines. <u>Interviews</u> can be easier to read than novels and short stories. You can usually read one front-to-back in 30 minutes or less.

irony—*n.* the use of words that mean the opposite of what you mean. A good example is when you say "Gee, I can't wait to go to the dentist and get those cavities filled" in a sarcastic tone, when going to the dentist is obviously the last thing you want to do.

jargon—*n.* specialized, technical language. My mom writes instruction books for home electronics. Her job is to translate technical <u>jargon</u> into plain English so people can set up their DVD players.

literal—*adj.* the real, dictionary meaning. What a word or phrase or any kind of writing or speaking actually means. "Go jump in a lake" doesn't usually mean someone wants you to get wet. But the <u>literal</u> meaning of the phrase is exactly that—go take a leap into the nearest pond, buddy.

Whiz Quiz

Identify the part of speech of the following words:
blonde
threaten
fake
mambo

metaphor—*n.* figurative use of words in which a word or phrase is used to mean something other than what it usually means. As you can probably tell by now, the English Language Arts are all about using words in creative ways, just like the fine arts are about using paint and clay in creative ways. For a creative writer, <u>metaphors</u> are as important as paint is for an artist. In my screenplay *Pretty Dumb*, I use metaphors all the time. Here are a couple: Fabio was a filmmaking *machine*, churning out two to three movies a year. Pamela's career was in *overdrive*. Every part she wanted, she got. (See the definition for *simile*— it's a lot *like* <u>metaphor</u>.)

motivation—*n.* in English language arts, it is the reason a character does something. Tests often ask you to identify a character's <u>motivation</u>. *Example*: In my screenplay for *Pretty Dumb*, James King ended up talking about Pamela Anderson behind her back. What was James's <u>motivation</u>? To answer that, you would look for the part of the story that made James trash Pamela.

narrative—*n.* a story. The <u>narrative</u> in *Pretty Dumb* follows two actresses as they angle for the starring role in a romantic comedy starring Jim Carrey.

omniscient—*adj.* all-knowing. This word is usually used in the phrase "<u>omniscient</u> narrator," which is a narrator in a story who "knows" everything that is going on and shares that information with the reader.

paraphrase—*v.* to express something using different words. Tests often ask you to <u>paraphrase</u> a story or a character's views. That just means write down what happened in the story or what a character thinks in a few sentences. I have to be able to paraphrase my screenplay *Pretty Dumb* in just a few words when I go try to sell it to Hollywood. Here it goes: Three days, two blonde actresses, one juicy movie role.

parody—*n.* a humorous mockery. <u>Parodies</u> mimic "normal" writing genres like horror, mystery, and romance. A good movie example of a <u>parody</u> is *The Pink Panther* series, starring Peter Sellers, from the 1960s and '70s. It is a parody of "normal" detective movies. Watch it—you will laugh and laugh and laugh.

personification—*n.* giving a thing human attributes. *Example*: "New York City moves to the beats of a million different drummers." New York doesn't move at all to any drummer. It just sits there. <u>Personification</u> makes the city "like a person."

persuade—*v.* to convince. Writers will often try to <u>persuade</u> readers that their point of view is correct. Tests often ask you to figure out what the writer is trying to <u>persuade</u> you to think. I am <u>persuading</u> you to learn the word <u>persuade</u>. <u>Persuaded</u>?

plagiarism—*n.* the act of stealing someone else's writing and claiming it as your own. Don't do it. You'll get in trouble.

WhizQuiz

Write the following sentences using **metaphors**:

Pam is fast.

James is confused.

Fabio likes ice cream a lot.

WhizTip

A good way to remember **narrative** is to think of the word **narrator**: the person who tells a story.

WhizTip

You can remember **paraphrase** by thinking of the word "phrase." You are replacing a long piece of writing with a simple phrase.

WhizTip

A good way to remember **personification** is to think of the word "person." You are describing an object as you would a person.

English Language Arts

point of view—*n*. one way of looking at things. A character's point of view is that character's way of thinking. For example, in my screenplay *Pretty Dumb*, it is James King's point of view that Pamela Anderson is too old for the female lead in a Jim Carrey movie. Pamela Anderson's point of view is that James King is a silly supermodel who would make the Jim Carrey movie a disaster. Each tries to persuade the movie's director, Fabio, that her point of view is the correct one.

premise—*n*. the basis for a story. The premise of my screenplay *Pretty Dumb* is two blonde actresses are gunning for the same part, and the person who decides who gets the part, Fabio, is evil.

preposition—*n*. a word that relates a noun or a pronoun to the other words in the sentence. Some popular prepositions are: *by, at, to, with, in, for, from*. What's that spell? BATWIFF. (You swing the batt, you whiff.) Cherish it. Remember it.

preview—*n*. an advance showing. When I go to the movies, my favorite part is the movie previews before the feature presentation. Why? The previews are always good, but the feature presentation is not always good.

progression—*n*. movement forward toward a goal. It is good if your grades show a steady progression upwards. If you are getting lots of Cs, try to start a progression up to Bs, and then to As.

propaganda—*n*. the kind of writing that a government or group uses to get you to believe something. Propaganda is used all the time during wars, in which one country tells its citizens that the other country is the worst country in the world. And the other country has propaganda that says the same thing about the first country. In propaganda, the facts aren't important—it is convincing readers that is important.

relevant—*adj*. pertaining to the matter at hand. Tests often tell you to "consider the relevant information" before choosing your answer. You can remember what relevant means by thinking of the word "related." Relevant information is "related" to the answer.

simile—*n*. a comparison of unlike things that uses the words *like* or *as*. James is crazy like a fox. Pamela is smart as a whip. (By the way—those examples are both also clichés.)

speculate—*v*. to think about; to guess at. You are often asked to speculate as to why a character did what he did. That means you need to think about who that character is and why he would do what he did. *Example*: If you are asked to speculate as to why James King got a part in a movie and Pamela Anderson didn't, you would have to look at the part, why James would be good for it, and why Pamela would not.

summarize—*n*. to create a short recap of the main points of a story. One of the main things you do in English class is summarize what you read. The best way to write a <u>summary</u> is to recap the story in the order things happened, so you don't forget anything.

suspense—*n.* the state of not knowing what will happen (otherwise known as the thing that puts you on the edge of your seat). Writers use <u>suspense</u> all of the time to keep you turning the pages. If you already know what's going to happen, why read on? In my screenplay, I use <u>suspense</u> the whole way—you don't find out who gets the part in the Jim Carrey movie until the very end.

symbolism—*n.* the use of an object to stand for something that can't be seen. For example, there are a lot of memorials in Washington, DC, that <u>symbolize</u> the soldiers who lost their lives in our wars. Writers use <u>symbolism</u> when they need to say something without really saying it. An example of this is when a writer <u>symbolizes</u> the passing of seasons by following a leaf as it falls from a tree and then decays on the ground, then feeds the roots of the tree it fell from.

synonym—*n.* a word that means the same thing as another word. *Daring* and *adventurous* are <u>synonyms</u>. *Timid* and *cowardly* are <u>synonyms</u>. When you are writing, instead of using the same word over and over, try to use <u>synonyms</u> to change things up a little bit. So if you use the word *car* in the first sentence, use *automobile* in the second and *vehicle* in the third.

timeline—*n.* a graphical representation of a chronology; a bunch of dates in chronological order on a line. <u>Timelines</u> are all over tests. Sometimes you have to write a story from a <u>timeline</u>. Sometimes you have to read a timeline to see what happened in what order. Here's an example from my screenplay:

Whiz Quiz

Write a one-sentence summary of the last book you read.

_____
_____
_____
_____

Related Word

synonymous—adj. having the same meaning, but in a larger sense. Michael Jordan is synonymous with pro basketball. Ticker tape parades are synonymous with Yankee championships.

Pretty Dumb: Monday

10am—James meets with Fabio	3pm—Pamela goes on *Extra* and trashes James	7pm—James and Pamela get in a fight at the Golden Globes
9am—Pamela meets with Fabio	1pm—Pamela and James have lunch	5pm—James goes on *Access Hollywood* and trashes Pamela	11pm—Fabio has a late-night meeting with a mystery actress

transition—*n.* the process of moving from one part of a story to the next. The weirdest examples of <u>transitions</u> occur during local newscasts when the news anchor has to switch from some gruesome tale of violence to the weather report, like this: "In all, 679 people were seriously or critically injured in the massive earthquake. But that doesn't compare to the number of people who will be delighted with tomorrow's sunny forecast! And here to tell us about it is Steve Stevarino! Take it away, Stevester!"

valid—*adj.* sound. In my screenplay *Pretty Dumb*, Fabio the director has <u>valid</u> reasons to choose James King (she is a star on the rise) and Pamela Anderson (she is a better-known blonde actress). In the end, however, Fabio chooses to put Barbra Streisand in a blonde wig. The movie is a huge hit, Fabio and Barbra and Jim Carrey all win Oscars, and an angry James King and Pamela Anderson start plotting to ruin Fabio (the plot for *Pretty Dumb II*).

verifiable—*adj.* provable; able to be verified. Something that is <u>verifiable</u> is something that can be proved with facts. Your age is <u>verifiable</u>—you just have to show your birth certificate.

WhizWords

analyze
clarify
compare
contrast
evaluate
summarize

English Language Arts
Thinking Big

Lots of times when you're taking tests, you're asked to write down a date or name that you have memorized. These kinds of test questions basically test your memory. If you remember what you memorized, you'll be just fine.

But sometimes you have to do a little more than just remember. Sometimes you have to really think about a reading passage on a test, and figure out on your own what you think and how you should write it down. These kinds of questions ask you to **analyze** a problem, **evaluate** the situation, **summarize** a story, **compare and contrast** ideas, and **clarify** your answer.

When these words appear in test questions, some kids freeze because they know a lot is expected of them—at least a lot more than just writing down a simple definition for a Social Studies test or identifying a shape on a geometry test. A good way to stop yourself from freezing is to get used to **analyzing, evaluating, summarizing,** and **clarifying** in situations that aren't so scary.

One great way to build your vocabulary is to hear the words read aloud. So, until they make an audio version of this book, ask an adult to play an audio book you like when you are driving around. Your local library probably has lots of audio books, just like mine. I personally like to listen to the *Harry Potter* books.

GETTING DEEP EXERCISE
In this exercise you are going to think deep about shallow things that you know a lot about. First, go back to the English Language Arts WhizWords and refresh your memory about what the "Thinking Big" words mean. Now pick a movie star, TV star, or entertainer you actually like or know a lot about. I am going to use Britney Spears as my victim, er, subject.

Write your subject at the top of the page. Now write down our six "getting deep" words along the left side of a piece of paper, about five lines apart. Next to each word, write down a topic relating to your victim, er, subject. Then write a short paragraph that answers the "questions" you have written. Here's mine:

Britney Spears
Analyze her album, *Oops . . . I Did It Again.*
Evaluate her singing.
Summarize why she is so popular.
Clarify her relationship with Justin Timberlake.
Compare and contrast Britney Spears and Christina Aguilera.

Once you have done this with one subject, pick another one and do it again. Keep practicing and you'll get really good at this. The more you see and use these words, the more comfortable you will get with them, and the better you'll do on your tests.

On the Test
Which is the best summary of this passage?

WhizWords

analogy
figurative language
flashback
foreshadow
imagery
irony
metaphor
personification
simile
symbolism

English Language Arts
Writers' Tools

Good writers know how to use all sorts of tools to keep readers' eyes glued to the page (that's a **metaphor**, by the way). Some writers are so good at it, you just can't stop reading. I keep a flashlight under my bed for nights when my parents tell me to turn out my light and go to sleep, but I just can't stop reading. Good writers make writing look easy, so you don't notice all of the tools they are using.

But on tests, it's important to be able to pick out the tools writers use. Lots of reading questions on tests ask you to identify things like **metaphors, symbolism**, and **analogies**—basically all of the words that I have listed at the top of this page. The only way to learn how to find all of these things is to practice finding them in the stories you read every day.

IDENTIFYING A WRITER'S TOOLS EXERCISE

You are going to have to do a little hunting and gathering for this exercise. I want you to go through your house and get on the Internet and find examples of the following types of stories:

Newspaper—sports story
Magazine—fashion story
Internet (print one out)—movie review
Newspaper—article from the editorial page
Internet (print one out)—piece of short fiction
Magazine—celebrity profile
Newspaper—political story

Gather these up in one place. Now, over the next week, I want you to read one of these stories every day and:

1. Underline the writers' tools.
2. Write the writer's tool in the margin.

There probably won't be enough room in the margins for some of these. If there isn't, you can write down the writer's tools you identify on Post-It Notes and stick them to the story.

English Language Arts
Adverbs and Adjectives

Imagine a world made up of only nouns and verbs. Actors would be . . . just actors. Not *terrible* actors, not *handsome* actors, not *overpaid* actors . . . just actors. Singers would be . . . just singers. Not *gorgeous* singers or *overproduced* singers or singers with voices that only a mother could love. Just . . . singers.

Luckily we have **adverbs** and **adjectives**, the words that make life special! Derek Jeter is the best shortstop in the league with a *sweet* swing, *nimble* feet and *soft* hands. The New York Yankees are *perennial* champions with *incredible* talent and *limitless* potential.

Yes, **adjectives** and **adverbs**, the simple modifiers of verbs, nouns and other **adjectives** and **adverbs**, give writing its spice. So it is very important to use them when you write. It makes your writing more interesting to read, which gets you better grades on your papers and writing tests. All good things, wouldn't you say?

WRITING YOUR AUTOBIOGRAPHY EXERCISE

If you don't believe me, let me prove it. I want you to try to describe your own life without adjectives and adverbs. Then I want you to describe your life WITH adjectives and adverbs—as many as you can possibly think of.

That's right—it's autobiography time. Grab a pencil and paper. Start by filling out this general outline. Write down three events in each age bracket you will write about in your own journal or notebook. Stuff like losing your first tooth, learning to swim, moving to a new town, joining the basketball team—events that are memorable and important to you.

Age

0 – 4

_____

5 – 8

_____

9 – present

_____

Now write two versions of your autobiography: 1) using no adverbs or adjectives; 2) using as many adverbs and adjectives as you can think of. Underline the adjectives and adverbs in the second version when you are done. I have provided you with a few adjectives and adverbs that you can use if you get stumped.

Adjectives and
adverbs for your
autobiography
goofy
fast
unbelievable
slow
smelly
late
first
early
straight
green
gawky
crazy
funny
laughable
smart
right
heavenly
regrettable

Chapter 2

Social Studies

Related Word

abolish—v. to get rid of.

abolitionist—*n.* someone who fought against slavery. When this country had slavery, there were a bunch of <u>abolitionists</u> trying to free the slaves. Some gave speeches, some ran the underground railroad—all of the <u>abolitionists</u> were working to stop a terrible system.

acculturation—*n.* the modification of one culture when it is exposed to another. When people from other countries emigrate to America, they go through a process of <u>acculturation</u> in which their "home" culture is influenced by American culture.

adapt—*v.* to change in response to other changes. The word is often used to describe how people and animals <u>adapt</u> as the environment changes. Charles Darwin found that animals <u>adapt</u> to their environments.

adversary—*n.* the enemy! President George W. Bush's <u>adversary</u> in the 2000 presidential election was Al Gore.

aggressor—*n.* the person or country who attacks first. Germany was the <u>aggressor</u> in World War II.

industrial—adj. pertaining to an economy based on industry (building things).

agrarian—*adj.* pertaining to a culture or economy based on farming and agriculture. The U.S. went from an <u>agrarian</u> economy in the 1800s to an industrial economy and 1900s. Now there are hardly any farmers left.

allegiance—*n.* a deep commitment to something, like your country or your family. Of course, we have all pledged <u>allegiance</u> to the flag in school.

alliance—*n.* an association of people or nations coming together to achieve a common goal. Think of the TV show *Survivor*—the players try to form <u>alliances</u> to protect themselves from getting voted off the show.

ambition—*n.* a burning desire to achieve a goal or to become something. The singer Madonna is often noted for her <u>ambition</u> to become famous. She doesn't have much singing talent, just tons of <u>ambition</u>. The same can be said of lots of actors and politicians.

WhizList

amendment—*n*. a change to the Constitution. We have had 27 <u>amendments</u> since the Constitution was adopted in 1789.

animism—*n*. a belief system that puts control of natural phenomena, like the weather, in control of a higher power. In an animist culture, people often pray to the gods of various natural phenomena, like the "god of rain" or the "god of summer."

anthropology—*n*. the study of cultures. If you become an <u>anthropologist</u>, you will learn all about the thousands of different cultures that humans have formed.

antitrust—*adj*. opposing business monopolies. <u>Antitrust</u> laws in the United States are supposed to keep one company from controlling an entire industry. Recently, Microsoft was found to be a monopoly controlling the software industry, and was ordered to break up into smaller companies.

artifact—*n*. a tool or weapon from an ancient culture. I actually found an <u>artifact</u> myself when my family went camping in the Adirondack Mountains last year. I was digging for worms to use for fish bait when I found an arrowhead!

assert—*v*. to claim; to insist. The colonies <u>asserted</u> their independence from England. They just went and claimed it, no questions asked. During the civil rights movement, African Americans <u>asserted</u> their right to vote. In the '70s, feminists <u>asserted</u> their right to equal pay for equal work. As citizens, we <u>assert</u> our rights to do things all the time—no one can stop us. Yes, you could call this country <u>Assert</u>america if you wanted!

assimilate—*v*. to make similar or to absorb into a system or culture. This word is often used when discussing how immigrants are absorbed into American culture. <u>Assimilation</u> is a complex process. Immigrants come here with their own customs. They want to keep some customs, but they also need to adopt some American customs. So the country <u>assimilates</u> them, but it is never easy.

assumption—*n*. a statement that's accepted to be true without

On the Test
The first ten amendments to the U.S. Constitution are called the Bill of Rights.

DOUBLE MEANING
assimilate—v. to break food down into its nutrients and absorb it (science).

21

actual proof that it's true. When I start out each day, it is with the assumption that it's going to be a great day! That assumption is not always accurate.

austerity—*n.* forced economy or strictness. When a country goes to war, its citizens often have to practice austerity, so there are more resources available for the war effort.

benevolent—*adj.* kind; caring. Most often used when talking about a "benevolent dictator," which means the dictator has total power, but he uses it for good, not evil. Superman would be a benevolent dictator.

Whiz Tip

One way to remember benevolent is to imagine a nice person named Ben: like Ben Franklin or Ben Affleck.

bias—*n.* prejudice. It usually means thinking someone is less than you are for a reason that doesn't make any sense, like gender or skin color. That is bias, or prejudice.

bicameral—*adj.* made of two legislative bodies. The United States has a bicameral legislature made of the House of Representatives and the Senate.

boom and bust economy—*n.* a kind of economy where things go incredibly well for a while, then crash and go incredibly poorly from there on out. It is most often used to describe the California gold rush in the 1800s, when everyone flocked to California for the boom, but once everyone was there and all of the gold had been mined, it all went bust.

boycott—*v.* to refuse to have dealings with a company or country because you disagree with something it does. It is a peaceful way to protest. Instead of picketing or doing something violent, people can boycott. Martin Luther King convinced black people to boycott the Montgomery, Alabama bus system to protest segregation on the buses. That meant no black people would ride the buses, which meant the buses lost a lot of money. So then they had to pay attention to what Martin Luther King said, or they would go out of business.

buffalo soldiers—*n.* black soldiers who fought against the Native Americans during westward expansion. The Native Americans gave them the name buffalo soldiers because of the courage they displayed in battle.

DOUBLE MEANING
capital—n.
the city where a state or nation's government is located.

capital—*n.* in economics, it means the wealth used to create more wealth. Basically, capital is money or property. If you were going to start a dot-com company, you would need some capital to start with—that includes money to pay for your staff, a place to work, and some computers to work on.

capitalist—*n.* in economics, it is the person who owns the wealth used to create more wealth. Donald Trump is a famous capitalist.

carpetbagger—*n.* a politician who runs for office in a state she is not from. Most recently, Hillary Rodham Clinton was called a <u>carpetbagger</u> when she ran for Senate in New York, even though she was not from New York and had never lived here before.

censorship—*n.* restriction on what someone can say or do. Although the First Amendment to the Constitution protects our right to freedom of speech, television shows are <u>censored</u>, movies are <u>censored</u>, and songs are <u>censored</u>. It happens every day in this country—usually to protect young people from adult language and situations. Many artists and performers are frustrated by <u>censorship</u> in the United States. Some countries, however, <u>censor</u> everyone on what they can say anywhere, anytime. This type of <u>censorship</u> is used to control people and prevent them from complaining about the government.

centralized—*adj.* focused in one person or area. In Social Studies, the word is usually used to talk about governments. A <u>centralized</u> government gives a lot of power to one person or group of people—like a king or a single ruling party. A <u>decentralized</u> government spreads that power out to a lot of people or groups of people.

checks and balances—*n.* when talking about the U.S. government, it is the system of government branches that each limit one another's power. So the president can do some things, but Congress has a say in what he does. Same with Congress—it can do some things, but the president also has a say. The judiciary branch—the courts—has a say in everything, too, and Congress and the president have a say in who gets to be a judge.

civic—*adj.* relating to your city or town. This word is sometimes used when discussing your role as a citizen. People often say "It's your <u>civic</u> duty to vote." That just means that as a member of a community, you should take part in what is going on there.

civil disobedience—*n.* a kind of protest where someone refuses to obey civil laws because she doesn't believe in them. <u>Civil disobedience</u> is almost always nonviolent. Martin Luther King organized sit-ins to protest "whites-only" restaurants. Black people would simply sit at a table and not leave until the cops came and arrested them.

coerce—*v.* to force someone to do something by threatening him. I was <u>coerced</u> into babysitting for my sister last weekend—my dad said if I didn't, I wouldn't get the new PlayStation—ever! You may have heard about the <u>Coercive Acts</u> that England forced on the American colonies (called the Intolerable Acts by the colonists) after the Boston Tea Party.

colonize—*v.* to establish a culture in a foreign land by putting some citizens there. It often results in those citizens taking

WhizFact

The term carpetbagger was used to describe Northerners who moved South after the Civil War with nothing but the contents of their carpet-bags (suitcases) to take advantage of the post-war chaos to enter politics.

On the Test

From the passage, give three examples of a citizen's civic responsibilities.

WhizFact

The American writer Henry David Thoreau is the one who coined the term civil disobedience in the late 19th century.

Social Studies

over that foreign land. It's not a very nice thing to do, but it has been a common practice for many countries, including the United States.

commerce—*n.* the act of buying and selling things. When you go to Wal-Mart and buy a notebook, you are engaging in commerce, and so is Wal-Mart.

commodity—*n.* something that is bought or sold. Like a notebook or a car or a ton of grain. They are all commodities.

communism—*n.* a system where the people own the factories, farms, and other property. At least that is the communist ideal. In most communist countries so far—like Cuba and the old Soviet Union—the government "owns" the property and most of the people have little say in how everything is run.

compensation—*n.* the amount paid for goods (stuff) or services (labor). When you get paid for doing something, you are getting compensation. When you pay for something, you are giving compensation.

compromise—*n.* a settlement where each side gives up something. So if you want to watch TV after dinner but your dad wants you to wash the dishes, a compromise would be watching TV, and then washing the dishes afterward.

concession—*n.* something that is given up. When I wanted to switch bedrooms with my big sister Hillary, I offered a series of concessions: I would do her laundry, I would bow low whenever she came into a room, and I would give her my dessert for a whole year. She didn't budge.

confiscate—*v.* to take away. Once my parents confiscated my PlayStation for one month because I got three straight Cs in English class.

conscription—*n.* the policy of forcing citizens to fight in wars. It's also called the draft. At different points in history, America has conscripted people into the armed forces, usually when there was a war on. At other times, the armed forces have been made up of volunteers.

consensus—*n.* general agreement. After my sister Hillary refused to switch bedrooms with me, I tried to form a consensus among the rest of my family (parents, grandparents, cousins, uncles, aunts) that I deserved her room. While I succeeded, and they agreed with me, she still wouldn't budge.

consent—*n.* permission. In Social Studies, it is often used to describe elected officials serving at the "consent of the governed." That means we put them in office by voting for them, and we can get rid of them if we want.

consequences—*n.* the results of something that happened. As

24

a parent or teacher must have told you at some point in your life, there are <u>consequences</u> for your actions. In Social Studies, the word is usually used when talking about something bad that happened, like Japan bombing Pearl Harbor (<u>consequence</u>: the U.S. joined the war) or the Watergate scandal (<u>consequence</u>: Nixon resigned). But <u>consequences</u> can also stem from positive events.

constitution—*n.* the laws that govern a group of people, usually a country or state. The U.S. <u>Constitution</u> has in it the basic laws that we follow in this country.

controversy—*n.* a situation where two sides have opposing views, and people have a hard time figuring out who is right. There was a huge <u>controversy</u> at my school last year when my friend Ralph refused to wear the new uniform—and his parents agreed with him! The principal called an assembly, Ralph's parents were in and out of school almost every day, Ralph was suspended, and it was in the newspaper!

corrupt—*v.* marked by dishonesty. The history of the United States is filled with <u>corrupt</u> politicians—politicians who took bribes to get laws passed.

covenant—*n.* a binding agreement; a compact. It's basically promising something, cross-your-heart, hope to die, stick a needle in your eye. A serious promise.

currency—*n.* a country's money. Our <u>currency</u> is dollars, the British use pounds, and the Japanese use yen.

democracy—*n.* a government where the people hold the power. We have a representative <u>democracy</u>, which means we elect representatives to do what we, the people, want them to do.

deprive—*v.* to take away. In Social Studies, the word is often used to talk about people being <u>deprived</u> of their rights. That means they don't have any rights to do what they want to do. When my friend Ralph's parents were against the dress code, they said Ralph was being <u>deprived</u> of his right to dress how he wants.

despotism—*n.* rule by a despot, someone who has absolute power and can do whatever he wants. Hitler was a <u>despot</u> in Germany. Saddam Hussein is a <u>despot</u> in Iraq. There are still lots of <u>despots</u> around the world.

detente—*n.* the relaxing of tensions between nations. After the Cold War between the United States and Russia ended in the 1990s, the countries have been enjoying a period of <u>detente</u>.

deter—*v.* to prevent; to stop. My mom doesn't understand why Britney Spears' mom doesn't try to <u>deter</u> her from wearing those skimpy outfits.

diffuse—*v.* in Social Studies, the spreading of one culture

The Mayflower Compact was a covenant signed by the 41 male passengers on the Mayflower, saying they would stick together.

To remember despotism, think of the word "despicable."

throughout another. When people from another country immigrate to the United States, they usually eventually <u>diffuse</u> through the country, spreading out through the land.

diplomat—*n.* a person who represents her country while living in another country. Most countries have <u>diplomats</u> in other countries, so if something happens, say, in Mexico, the United States' <u>diplomat</u> in Mexico can make sure the United States' interests are kept in mind.

discriminate—*v.* to treat someone badly for unfair reasons. Black people have been <u>discriminated</u> against a lot in our country. Even my favorite sport, baseball, <u>discriminated</u> against black people until 1947, when Jackie Robinson became the first black man in the Major Leagues. And racial <u>discrimination</u> still exists—there may be tons of black players, but there are hardly any black managers.

dissent—*n.* disagreement. In America, you have the right to register your <u>dissent</u>, no matter what you think. It's called freedom of speech. My friend Ralph's parents had every right to register their <u>dissent</u> with the school's dress code. They lost—Ralph had to wear the uniform like the rest of us, but they still had the right to disagree.

diversity—*n.* variety. In Social Studies, the word is usually used to talk about the <u>diversity</u> of opinions (lots of different opinions) and the <u>diversity</u> of cultures (lots of different cultures) that make up America. Some call our <u>diversity</u> a melting pot, some call it a quilt—the point is, we have a very <u>diverse</u> society.

domestic—*adj.* having to do with home. In Social Studies, you may hear the phrase "<u>domestic</u> affairs"—that refers to issues within a country, not in other countries.

dominate—*v.* to take precedence; to be most important. Combining the definition above with this one, you may have heard of "domestic affairs <u>dominating</u> Congress" or something along those lines. That means issues close to home are taking up most of the time and effort in Congress. Different issues tend to <u>dominate</u> in our culture, depending on all sorts of things: war and peace, the economy, the rights of people being respected or abused. All of these issues have <u>dominated</u> at one time or another.

due process—*n.* the established way our court system works. The phrase "You have a right to <u>due process</u>" is very important in this country. It means no matter who you are, you get treated the same—and fairly—in our court system.

economy—*n.* the combination of goods, services, and people and how they all work together to survive. We have a market <u>economy</u>, which means the laws of supply and demand determines who makes and gets what. The other kind of <u>economy</u> is a command <u>economy</u>, where a government determine (commands) who makes and gets what. China has a command <u>economy</u>.

eloquent—*adj.* good at public speaking. If you are a politician, it helps to be <u>eloquent</u>, since you have to make so many speeches all the time. John F. Kennedy was an <u>eloquent</u> speaker; so were Ronald Reagan and Bill Clinton. But I think the most <u>eloquent</u> speaker I know is the Rock on WWF. That guy can really hold an audience!

emancipation—*n.* the act of gaining freedom. Our <u>emancipation</u> from England and the <u>emancipation</u> of slaves in our country are two pivotal moments in our history.

embargo—*n.* the prohibition of goods from entering or leaving a country. After the Gulf War, the United States put an oil <u>embargo</u> on Iraq so they couldn't sell oil to anyone anymore.

emigrate—*v.* to leave one's home country for another. This country is made up of millions of people who have <u>emigrated</u> from distant lands to find opportunity here. Orlando Hernandez is a Yankee pitcher who <u>emigrated</u> from Cuba under difficult circumstances.

empathy—*n.* identification with someone else's situation. I really want my sister's bedroom. I tried to get her to feel <u>empathy</u> for me because I have a postage stamp of a bedroom compared to her humongous bedroom. She laughed, then punched me hard in the shoulder.

enforce—*v.* to make sure something takes place. Most often used in the phrase "<u>enforce</u> our laws" and "<u>enforce</u> our borders." It just means if we say we are going to do something, we will do it. My parents <u>enforce</u> their home rules by grounding me and taking away things when I break the rules.

enlighten—*v.* to inform. My sister <u>enlightened</u> me about why I would never get her room: she is bigger, stronger, and older, and couldn't care less how small my room is.

entrepreneur—*n.* someone who takes business risks in a capitalist economy. It can be someone who bets that if she is right about a business venture, she will get rich. <u>Entrepreneurs</u> start most of the new companies in our country every year, betting each business will succeed. Steve Jobs was an <u>entrepreneur</u> when he started Apple Computer in his garage in the 1970s. Martha Stewart took an ability to make pretty doilies and turned it into a multi-million dollar empire! Smart.

escapism—*n.* the act of escaping from reality by using fantasy. Since my sister told me I would never get her room, I have been using <u>escapism</u> to cope. In my fantasy, I imagine her getting all

Whiz Tip

The U.S. is called "the land of the free," so emancipation (freedom) is probably our most important ideal. That means you are lucky—but it also means lots of test questions on the subject.

Whiz Tip

Think of "using force" to remember the word enforce.

Social Studies

Fs, getting sent to boarding school far, far away, and me getting her room.

ethnocentrism—*n*. belief that one's ethnic group is better than all the others. Ethnocentrism is a leading cause of wars.

evolve—*v*. to improve over time. Scientists believe humans evolved from apes. My mother hopes I will evolve into a cleaner person. I will admit that my personal hygiene is a bit of a problem.

executive branch—*n*. the branch of government that administers the country. The president is the head of the executive branch.

expansionism—*n*. the policy of taking over additional land and countries. The United States had an expansionist policy. That's how it grew from 13 to 50 states.

expedition—*n*. an adventurous trip. To expand as fast as it did, the U.S. needed a lot of people to go out on expeditions into uncharted territory.

fascism—*n*. a government with a ruthless dictator, centralized control, and nationalist tendencies. Hitler was a fascist. So was Mussolini. The Allied Powers fought fascism in World War II and won. It's all my great-grandfather talks about!

federalism—*n*. a government with separate states that are united under one larger government. The United States (get it—*united* states) is a federalist system. Alexander Hamilton was an advocate of federalism.

feminism—*n*. a movement committed to getting women the same rights and opportunities as men. Women make less money than men for the same work, and our society treats them differently in many ways. Feminists are out to change that so everyone is equal.

fiscal—*adj*. pertaining to finances. This word is most often used in the phrase "fiscal policy." Fiscal policy is a government's plan for how it gets and spends its money.

forfeit—*v*. to give up; to hand over. When someone commits a crime and goes to jail, he forfeits a lot of his rights as a citizen, like the freedom to walk around and go wherever he wants. If your baseball team doesn't show up for a game, it forfeits the game and loses automatically. That happened to my team when our bus broke down.

free enterprise—*n*. an economic system in which businesses can try to make a profit without the government getting in their way with lots of regulations. The United States has a free enterprise system.

WhizFact
Gloria Steinem and Betty Friedan are famous modern feminists. Elizabeth Cady Stanton is a famous suffragette—a woman who fought for women's right to vote in the early 20th century (see definition for suffrage).

frontier—*n.* an area of land where people don't live yet; the great unknown. The United States was once just a few states on the East Coast with a great <u>frontier</u> to its west that still "belonged" to the Native Americans. If you're a *Star Trek* fan, you've heard William Shatner say these words a million times: "Space—the final <u>frontier</u> . . . . These are the voyages of the Starship Enterprise. It's five-year mission: to explore strange new worlds, to seek out new life and new civilizations, to boldly go where no man has gone before." That's exactly how the pioneers felt when they packed up their covered wagons and headed out West.

fundamental—*adj.* basic. In this country we have certain <u>fundamental</u> rights—the rights to life, liberty, and the pursuit of happiness. Maybe you've heard of these somewhere?

futile—*adj.* useless. Lots of times people will tell you not to try, that trying is <u>futile</u>. My sister keeps saying that about me trying to get her bedroom.

galvanize—*v.* to spur to action. A politician tries to <u>galvanize</u> the voting public in favor of her policies. That is a politician's job.

genocide—*n.* the planned killing of an entire group of people. Hitler's Nazis practiced <u>genocide</u> against the Jews. The United States practiced <u>genocide</u> against Native Americans.

grievances—*n.* complaints. The colonists had a list of <u>grievances</u> against mother England, the biggest of which was they were getting taxed a lot. I have a list of <u>grievances</u> I gave to my mother last week, the biggest of which was my allowance needs to be higher. The colonists rebelled. I hope my mom gets the hint.

idealist—*n.* one who is more influenced by ideals than by practicalities. An <u>idealist</u> wants to do what is right no matter how hard or impractical it may be.

immigration—*n.* the act of coming from a foreign country to live in a new country. America has grown in population over the years mainly due to <u>immigration</u>. The country practically begged people to <u>immigrate</u> here so it could push west over the frontier and fill up all of its land with new citizens.

impartial—*adj.* fair. Judges and juries are supposed to be <u>impartial</u>. That means they just go by the facts. Like Judge Judy on TV—she is an <u>impartial</u> judge who listens to all the facts, then she reams the person who is guilty.

impeachment—*n.* charging an elected official with doing something wrong. President Clinton was <u>impeached</u> a few years ago. It was only the second time in the history of the country a president was impeached. Clinton's impeachment hearings dominated the news for weeks.

List three things you once thought were futile:

1. _____
2. _____
3. _____

On the Test

How many immigrants came to the United States between 1820 and 1829?

Who was the first president to be impeached? Hint: It wasn't Bill Clinton.

Social Studies

imperialism—*n.* rule by an empire. A few hundred years ago, imperialism was the way to go. There was the Roman Empire, the Spanish Empire, and the German Empire. These imperial governments would go out and conquer a bunch of countries so they could expand their empires. Of course America was part of the British Empire—imperial Britain—at one point.

DOUBLE MEANING
impose—v. to butt in. You may have heard people say "I don't mean to impose, but . . ." and then they go ahead and impose.

impose—*v.* to force. My Spanish teacher imposed a "no English" rule last week in class, so no one could speak English in her class the whole week! If you did, you had to put your head on your desk for five minutes. It was really funny watching everyone mess up and put their heads on their desks.

inalienable—*adj.* unable to be taken away; unable to be separated from. Most often linked to Americans' inalienable rights of life, liberty, and the pursuit of happiness. One way to remember this word is to think about the word "alien." Space aliens are beings from other planets. So something that is INalienable is something that is NOT something from another planet.

unalienable

inaugurate—*v.* to have a ceremony where a politician gets installed in office. George W. Bush was inaugurated in 2001 after a bitter election battle against Al Gore.

indigenous—*adj.* native. The people who are originally from a country are called the country's indigenous people. Native Americans are indigenous to North America—everyone else who lives in this country came here from somewhere else or is descended from someone who did.

industrialism—*n.* an economic system where big industries are most important. Industrialism dominated the United States in the 20th century.

inevitable—*adj.* going to happen; unavoidable. It is inevitable that you are going to have to take tests, so you might as well just get used to them. When something is unavoidable, my grandfather always says, "It's as inevitable as death and taxes." I have my own expression, "It's as inevitable as death, taxes, and the New York State tests."

inhabitants—*n.* people who live somewhere. You are an inhabitant of New York. Prince Charles is an inhabitant of England.

Related Word
innovate—v. to introduce something new.

innovation—*n.* a brand new way of doing something or a new device that is better than it used to be. The electric guitar was an innovation that allowed bands to play louder. Before the electric guitar, the only way to play loud was on an acoustic guitar aimed at a microphone. Boring!

instability—*n.* the state of being unsteady and insecure. When things are up in the air, when they can go one way or the other— that is instability. *Example*: There is instability on a baseball team when the players don't like the manager and the manager doesn't like the players. Who is right—the players who say the manager is stupid or the manager who says the players are terrible? Who do you side with? All these questions lead to <u>instability</u>. It's the same with a country when there is <u>instability</u>. Usually, there is <u>instability</u> when there is a change in leaders. Maybe the army liked the old leader better, so they won't listen to the new leader. That leads to <u>instability</u>.

institution—*n.* a really well known or well established organization or person. There are real <u>institutions</u> like colleges (<u>institutions</u> for higher learning) and hospitals (health <u>institutions</u>). There are also people who are known as <u>institutions</u>—Bill Cosby is a comedy <u>institution</u>, and Michael Jordan is a basketball <u>institution</u>. They are just SO IMPORTANT to their fields, they are <u>institutions</u>.

insurgent—*n.* a person who revolts against authority. When you watch newscasters, you may hear them talk about "rebel <u>insurgents</u>" in other countries, and then show some guys with machine guns running around in the woods fighting against government forces.

insurrection—*n.* revolt against the people in charge. The word is used in the Declaration of Independence to describe the king of England's treatment of the colonies: "He has excited domestic <u>insurrections</u> amongst us." That means the colonists thought the king was turning them against each other.

integration—*n.* the creation of one group by combining different groups; having people of all different races living together instead of apart. Our country was segregated—white people and black people were separated from each other—until the 1950s and 1960s, when segregation was made illegal. Now we are an <u>integrated</u> society—people of all races are allowed to live side by side.

integrity—*n.* honesty; trustworthiness. People who do what they say they are going to do have <u>integrity</u>. People who lie do not have <u>integrity</u>. I think Justin Timberlake has <u>integrity</u> for staying with 'N Sync, even though he could go solo and make millions.

interdependent—*adj.* relying or counting on each other. Countries are getting more and more <u>interdependent</u>. Lots of countries rely on us for corn; we rely on lots of countries for oil; and everyone relies on France for French fries.

intervene—*v.* to butt in. I had to <u>intervene</u> on the playground last week when my friend Ralph and that jerk Frankie got into a fight. I was able to keep them apart until the teacher came.

intolerant—*adj.* unable to accept views one doesn't agree with. There are lots of <u>intolerant</u> people in the world—people who don't like other people just because they are different. Don't be <u>intolerant</u>. It will just make you mean.

isolate—*v.* to separate from everything else. When I was in kindergarten, I was a big spaz. Sometimes I got so hyper my teacher had to <u>isolate</u> me at nap time—she put up big dividers so I couldn't see the rest of the kids and they couldn't see me.

jeopardy—*n.* peril; danger. Think of the game show *Jeopardy*. If you go on that show, you are in <u>jeopardy</u> of looking really stupid if you can't answer any questions.

judicial branch—*n.* the country's court system. One of three branches of the U.S. government, the <u>judicial branch</u> interprets the laws and hands down punishments.

jurisdiction—*n.* an area of authority. The word <u>jurisdiction</u> is often used to talk about the courts having <u>jurisdiction</u> over a case. That means the case happened in a court's physical area. So if someone robbed someone in Ulster County, the case would be tried in the <u>jurisdiction</u> of Ulster County.

laissez-faire—*adj.* favoring an economic doctrine that opposes government regulations. <u>Laissez-faire</u> economists think markets solve problems best, not governments.

lame duck—*n.* a politician who has some time left in her term, but her replacement has already been elected. So she is still doing her job, but she has already been voted out. That means she has no power, and she's basically just keeping the seat warm for her successor.

legislation—*n.* proposed laws. In the U.S. government, Congress writes and votes on <u>legislation</u>.

legislative branch—*n.* the branch of government that writes the laws. The U.S. has a bicameral <u>legislative branch</u> made up of the House of Representatives and the Senate.

loyalist—*n.* someone who is loyal to a leader or government. <u>Loyalists</u> who lived in the American colonies were against the colonies breaking from mother England.

mandate—*n.* the right to do something. In elections, when voters pick someone overwhelmingly, that politician has a <u>mandate</u>. That means the voters have told him—with their votes—that he can do what he wants because they agree with his plan. When a politician wins in a landslide, he has a <u>mandate</u> from the voters. When there is a close election (like when George W. Bush barely beat Al Gore in 2000), there is not a <u>mandate</u> because lots of people voted for the guy who lost.

mediate—*v.* to act as a peacemaker to solve a problem. My mom usually <u>mediates</u> the arguments between me and my sister.

WhizTip

To remember jurisdiction, **think of the word "jury."** A case's jurisdiction is wherever a jury would be seated to try the case.

WhizQuiz

Go to *www.house.gov* and find a piece of legislation Congress is working on now.

Related Word

landslide—n. winning an election by a huge margin.

My dad says he doesn't have the patience to mediate.

manifest destiny—*n.* a policy of imperialist expansion that says a country can take over another country because God says so. Imperialist countries like England took over other countries using this concept of manifest destiny. The United States took over lots of its western lands by using this concept of manifest destiny. Manifest destiny is bad. It's basically just an excuse to take over a country.

mercantilism—*n.* an economic system based on accumulating money, developing industry, establishing colonies, and trading. Mercantilism dominated Europe after feudalism fell.

mercenary—*n.* a professional soldier. Mercenaries fight for whomever pays them to fight. There's even a magazine for mercenaries called *Soldier of Fortune*. Get it? They *soldier* so they can make a *fortune*.

migration—*n.* the movement from one place to another. In the past 20 years, there has been a migration of people in this country from cold places like New York to warm places like Georgia.

militant—*adj.* combative; warring. Some countries have militant histories, ours included.

misconception—*n.* an incorrect assumption. My sister is under the misconception that I have given up trying to trade my tiny bedroom for her big bedroom. I have many more tricks up my sleeves.

moderate—*adj.* not extreme. Moderate temperatures are not too hot and not too cold. Moderate politicians are not too liberal and not too conservative.

municipal—*adj.* related to a city or a town. You probably have heard of a municipal government and a municipal school system and municipal courts. That just means those things are located in a city—whatever city that may be.

mutual—*adj.* shared in common between two people, things, or groups. When something is done for the mutual benefit, that means they both benefit. When Justin Timberlake and Britney Spears are seen in public together, they mutually benefit. All of her fans start to like him, and all of his fans start to like her.

nationalism—*n.* loyalty to one's country. Nationalism is a good thing when it means you really like your country and are proud of it. Nationalism is a bad thing when it means you really like your country but hate all the other countries. Most often these days, when you hear about nationalism, it's when one country is beating up on another one out of a feeling of nationalism.

DOUBLE MEANING
moderate—v. to manage a group of people who have different views.

WhizFact
The scientist Albert Einstein once said "Nationalism is an infantile sickness. It is the measles of the human race."

33

naturalization—*n.* the granting of citizenship to someone. The word is most often used when discussing the INS—the Immigration and <u>Naturalization</u> Service. That is the agency that helps people immigrate to this country and become citizens. A <u>naturalized</u> citizen is someone who immigrated here and became a citizen later.

negotiate—*v.* to discuss something with the goal of reaching an agreement. Throughout history there have basically been two ways to solve disagreements—to fight or to <u>negotiate</u>. <u>Negotiating</u> is better, because nobody gets hurt.

Name your nemesis!

nemesis—*n.* sworn enemy. The Joker is Batman's <u>nemesis</u>. Lex Luthor is Superman's <u>nemesis</u>. Christina Aguilera is Britney Spears' <u>nemesis</u>. Russia used to be the United States' <u>nemesis</u>.

impartial—adj. fair (see its definition).

neutral—*adj.* not taking sides. Lots of times, when two countries go to war, other countries remain <u>neutral</u>. That means they aren't taking sides in the war—they are staying out of it. The United States was <u>neutral</u> in World War II until Japan bombed Pearl Harbor.

nullify—*v.* to void; to take something back. Sometimes, after an agreement has been negotiated, something happens and the agreement gets <u>nullified</u>. That means all the negotiating was wasted, because the agreement that was reached doesn't count. It happens all the time in baseball when a team is trying to make a trade, but the trade gets <u>nullified</u> when one of the players doesn't pass his physical.

obstacle—*n.* something that gets in the way. You have probably been in a race through an <u>obstacle</u> course at some point. My main <u>obstacle</u> at school is that I have a hard time paying attention, but I'm working on it.

Name your favorite team's main opposition:

opposition—*n.* someone who is against someone else. It looks like the Yankees' main <u>opposition</u> as they try to get to the World Series is going to be the Seattle Mariners.

oppress—*v.* to keep somebody down. This country has a history of <u>oppressing</u> black people and women. That <u>oppression</u> isn't nearly as bad now as it used to be.

partisan—*n.* a supporter of a political party; a supporter of a cause. You have probably heard of "<u>partisan</u> politics" in Washington, DC. That means our two major political parties—the Democrats and Republicans—are more interested in getting their way than getting something done. Being a <u>partisan</u>—a supporter of their party—is more important than doing what they were elected to do.

persecute—*v.* to oppress. The Nazis <u>persecuted</u> Jews in World War II. The Romans <u>persecuted</u> Christians for hundreds of years. European colonists <u>persecuted</u> Native Americans for hundreds of years. Unfortunately, the history of mankind is filled with <u>persecution</u>.

petition—*n.* a formal request to a government or another authority. You have probably signed a <u>petition</u> at some point in your life. Last year I signed a <u>petition</u> to end the dress code at my school, but it didn't work—we still have a dress code!

pivotal—*adj.* the most important. The <u>pivotal</u> moment of my last baseball game was when the other team had the bases loaded and I struck out their best hitter. That's what I call <u>pivotal</u>.

polarize—*v.* to cause two groups to focus on their differences. The issue of slavery <u>polarized</u> the United States in the 1800s.

pragmatist—*n.* someone who is practical. A <u>pragmatist</u> tends to support things he thinks can actually be done. For example, a <u>pragmatist</u> would be satisfied if a last-place team just improved a little, and maybe the next year made it to the middle of the pack. He wouldn't expect the team to go from last place to first place in one year because that wouldn't be practical.

preservation—*n.* protection from destruction. This word is used most often when people are talking about <u>preserving</u> old buildings in their town (historic <u>preservation</u>) and when people are talking about preserving the environment (environmental <u>preservation</u>).

primary source—*n.* a first-hand record of an event. I was doing a report on how the pitcher Nolan Ryan got so good. Some of my <u>primary sources</u> were two letters that he wrote to his dad and tapes of three games he pitched way back in the 1970s.

principles—*n.* ideals; beliefs. A person who has <u>principles</u> is a person who does what she thinks is right, no matter what the consequences. Martin Luther King Jr. had <u>principles</u>. So did Che Guevara.

profit—*n.* in business, the money left over after you subtract the costs of making something that you sell. If it costs a company $20 to make a CD player and they sell it for $50, their <u>profit</u> is $30.

prohibit—*v.* to not allow; to forbid. Laws are basically created to <u>prohibit</u> bad behavior like drunk driving and stealing.

prosecute—*v.* to bring a legal case against someone. Famous people are always getting <u>prosecuted</u> for breaking the law. Puff Daddy got <u>prosecuted</u> for carrying an illegal weapon and bribing people. Jennifer Lopez was with him when he got arrested, but she didn't get <u>prosecuted</u>. I wonder why?

prosperity—*n.* success and riches. America is known for being a land of <u>prosperity</u>—there are a lot of people in this country who are rich and middle class. Many countries have no <u>prosper-</u>

WhizTip
To remember pivotal, think about "pivot" which means "to turn."

Antonym
idealist—n. a person who wants the best things possible to happen, no matter how impractical those things may be.

Related Word
self-preservation—n. the act of doing things that help you survive.

Related Word
prosperous—adj. rich.

35

ity at all—everyone is poor.

provoke—*v.* to anger; to egg on. Many animals are quite peaceful until they are <u>provoked</u>. Most bears won't even pay you any attention, but if you <u>provoke</u> them by poking them with a stick or shooting at them, you are in big trouble.

DOUBLE MEANING

public domain—n. books, articles, and products that aren't protected by a copyright. (Note: This book is NOT public domain!)

public domain—*n.* land that's owned by the state or government instead of by a person. Theoretically, that means all taxpayers "own" and can use the land. In the West, a lot of livestock graze on land that's <u>public domain</u>.

radical—*n.* someone who works for political or social revolution. Our country has a complicated relationship with <u>radicals</u>. When we were colonies breaking from England, we were the <u>radicals</u>, breaking the law. Now, as the most powerful nation in the world, we generally look down on <u>radicals</u>. And as a country based on the rule of law, revolution is not really our cup of tea. Just look at the famous <u>radicals</u> our country has had to see how complicated our relationship with them is.

WhizFact

Famous radicals include crazy writer Abbie Hoffman, presidential assassin Lee Harvey Oswald, and President Thomas Jefferson, who was a big fan of revolutions.

ramifications—*n.* the by-products of an event or act. My sister Hillary will be suffering several <u>ramifications</u> if she does not switch bedrooms with me, the first of which is: I will start calling her "Queen Doofus."

ratify—*v.* to pass. After a law is written, it has to be <u>ratified</u> by both houses of Congress—the House of Representatives and the Senate, before it is signed (or vetoed) by the president.

DOUBLE MEANING

ration—n. quantities of food.

ration—*v.* to give out in restricted amounts, usually during wartime, to conserve resources. Food and fuel are often rationed during wartime so more resources can be devoted to fighting the battles.

rebellion—*n.* a revolt against authority. Have you noticed how many words there are in this section that basically mean "revolt" and "rebel"? It is an important subject when it comes to the history of our country. <u>Rebellion</u> was involved when the colonies broke from England, and <u>rebels</u> have qualities that we as Americans value in a person. They do what they think is right, no matter what anyone thinks.

Reconstruction—*n.* the period after the Civil War when the South was controlled by the federal government, before those states were readmitted to the Union (1865-1877).

To remember Reconstruction, think of "reconstructing," or rebuilding, the country.

recruit—*v.* to get someone to join something. The most obvious use for this word is when people are talking about <u>recruiting</u> soldiers to join the armed forces. But people are also <u>recruited</u> to join the soccer team, the PTA, and to attend a particular college.

reform—*v.* to change for the better. One of the great things about our government is that if a law—or the government—

doesn't work, we can <u>reform</u> it by voting for representatives who want <u>reform</u>.

regional—*adj.* area-specific. My baseball team plays in a <u>regional</u> tournament every year—that's the tournament where all the teams from the New York City <u>region</u> play each other.

regulate—*v.* to limit. The government <u>regulates</u> all kinds of things. The most important may be the toxic emissions from cars and power plants. The government <u>regulates</u> the poisons in those emissions by setting limits the companies must not exceed. If the company doesn't follow those <u>regulations</u>, the company gets fined.

repeal—*v.* to take back; to rescind. Sometimes a law is <u>repealed</u> because is was really a bad, bad idea. One of the reasons the colonies broke from England was that England wouldn't <u>repeal</u> tax laws that were really hard on the colonies.

representation—*n.* the act of representing something or someone. In the phrase "taxation without representation," it means not having <u>representatives</u> in the government looking out for your interests. The main reason the colonies broke with England was that they were being taxed, but had no say at all in how much they were taxed and why.

republic—*n.* a government where the people elect representatives to do their bidding. The United States is a <u>republic</u>.

resolute—*adj.* firm; unwavering. I am <u>resolute</u> in my view that the New York Yankees are the best team in baseball, no matter what their actual record is.

restrain—*v.* to hold back. For example, I had to <u>restrain</u> my sister Hillary when my friend Ralph called her "Queen Doofus." She was quite angry. In American history, the New England <u>Restraining</u> Act was enacted by King Charles II in 1775. It <u>restrained</u> a handful of colonies from trading with anyone, and it made those colonies mad.

retaliation—*n.* the act of striking back after you get attacked. It is not good to start a fight, but sometimes you have to <u>retaliate</u> (see what my sister did in the definition above). Lincoln issued the Order of <u>Retaliation</u> in 1863 saying that if the South violated the rules of war by killing or enslaving captured Union soldiers, the Union would <u>retaliate</u> by doing the same to their soldiers.

revenue—*n.* money made. Government gets its <u>revenue</u> from taxes. Companies get their <u>revenue</u> by selling things. I get my <u>revenue</u> from my allowance and mowing lawns.

scarcity—*n.* lack. In wartime, there is often a <u>scarcity</u> of resources like rubber, steel, and fuel.

WhizQuiz

**List three
regulations at
your school:**

1. _____

2. _____

3. _____

Antonym

surrender—**v.
to give up.**

secede—*v.* to break away from a unit. The South *seceded* from the United States in 1861. That's what started the Civil War, because President Lincoln would not let them do it without a fight. The South's *secession* was a pivotal moment in this country's history.

secondary source—*n.* a summary or an account of an event or person. When I wrote my report on Nolan Ryan, the *secondary sources* I used included two *Sports Illustrated* articles on him and the biography they have on him at *majorleaguebaseball.com*.

sectionalism—*n.* excessive devotion to local customs. *Sectionalism* usually causes big problems between neighboring countries or states, because one group won't respect the other's point of view.

sedition—*n.* words or deeds causing people to rebel against the state. During wartime, acts of *sedition* are not tolerated. In 1798, the U.S. Congress passed the Alien and *Sedition* Acts to prevent political dissidents and the press from interfering with preparations for war with France.

Antonym

integration—n. the combination of groups of people.

segregation—*n.* the separation of people who are different. Blacks were *segregated* from white society for years in this country. In some churches, women and men are *segregated*, with women sitting on one side, men on the other. Boys are often *segregated* from girls in gym class. *Segregation* keeps people apart.

self-sufficient—*adj.* capable of providing for oneself. When my family went camping, I learned that I am not very *self-sufficient*. Without take-out restaurants and a comfortable mattress, I am pretty much useless.

siege—*n.* in war, a sustained attack. In World War I, troops were under a continuous state of *siege*. The fighting never stopped as the soldiers on both sides dug trenches and refused to give an inch.

sovereign—*n.* a king or queen. We don't have any sovereigns in our country. England still has its *sovereigns*, but they don't have any power anymore. They are just symbols of England's past.

stereotype—*n.* a judgment based on oversimple assumptions. You are using a *stereotype* when you think a person or group of people are a certain way for no real reason. Italian Americans are often *stereotyped* as being in the Mafia. Blonde women are often *stereotyped* as being ditzy. Obviously, a *stereotype* has nothing to do with an individual person. It's just a lazy way to form opinions of people.

WhizTip

To remember subversive means "undermining," remember sub means "under."

subversive—*adj.* undermining. As part of preparing for a war against France, Thomas Jefferson signed the Alien and Sedition

Acts which outlawed <u>subversive</u> behavior, like criticizing the government. Now we can criticize the government as much as we want.

succession—*n*. the process of following in order. There has been a <u>succession</u> of kings and queens in the history of most European nations. Sometimes the <u>succession</u> went smoothly. Sometimes, it was bloody.

suffrage—*n*. the right to vote. Women gained <u>suffrage</u> in this country in 1920. Eighteen-year-olds gained <u>suffrage</u> after the Vietnam War when they argued that if they could go to war, why couldn't they vote?

sympathizers—*n*. people who agree with something and want to help; people who are <u>sympathetic</u> to a person or a cause. Usually in American history, the word is used in the term "communist <u>sympathizers</u>," which means people who agreed with the communists and helped them out in the early 20th century.

tariffs—*n*. taxes on imports and exports. High <u>tariffs</u> on the colonies' imports and exports made colonists' mad at England. You know what happened next.

temperance—*n*. the act of not drinking alcohol. There was a <u>temperance</u> movement in the United States in the early 20th century that made drinking alcohol illegal. That was when gangsters like Al Capone made millions selling illegal booze.

topography—*n*. the physical aspects of a place or region. The word is often used in the phrase "<u>topographical</u> map," which is a map that shows a region's physical landscape instead of roads and landmarks.

totalitarianism—*n*. a type of government in which one person or party has absolute control. See my definition for *despotism* for more information (they're pretty much the same thing).

transcend—*v*. to surpass; to overcome. Sometimes you have to <u>transcend</u> your limitations to reach your goals. If your vocabulary is a limitation for you, this book should help you <u>transcend</u> that obstacle.

Treasury—*n*. the part of the government in charge of the money supply. Our <u>Treasury</u> Department makes sure there is enough, but not too much, money floating around to keep the economy moving.

unanimous—*adj*. being in complete agreement. In a <u>unanimous</u> decision, everyone votes the same way. 100 percent of the people vote the same way. When we took a vote from the students at school about our dress code, the students voted <u>unanimously</u> to repeal it.

urban—*adj*. related to the city. Lots of big cities around the

**To remember
suffrage,
remember
people "suffer"
when they don't
have the right
to vote.**

**Name a
limitation you
have had to
transcend in
your life:**

_____

_____

Related Word

majority—adj. In a
majority vote,
more than 50
percent of the
people vote one
way, but not
everybody.

Social Studies

rural—adj. related to the countryside.

country have been undergoing <u>urban</u> renewal, which means they are working to improve the quality of their inner cities and downtown areas.

utopia—*n.* a perfect world. Many systems of government promise their followers a <u>utopia</u> on Earth. I think Manhattan is the closest anyone has come to <u>utopia</u> yet!

verdict—*n.* a decision in a court case. It is the job of a jury to reach a <u>verdict</u> in a case. When members of a jury don't reach a <u>verdict</u>, it's called a "hung jury."

veteran—*n.* someone who has fought in a war. We celebrate <u>Veterans</u> Day to remember the people who have fought in all of our wars. My great-grandfather is a <u>veteran</u>—he fought in World War II.

veto—*n.* rejection of a proposal. In our government, a <u>veto</u> is a president's vote against legislation passed by Congress. Presidents often <u>veto</u> legislation they don't agree with.

viable—*adj.* possible. A "<u>viable</u> option" is an option that could work. However, in my quest to get my sister to switch her bedroom with me, I offered her many options I thought were <u>viable</u>. But none of them ended up working. So I am stuck in my little closet-sized room, while she lives in luxury.

WhizWords

communism
democracy
despotism
fascism
federalism
imperialism
republic
totalitarianism

Social Studies

Government

I was over at my great-grandfather's assisted living complex the other day, and he was going on and on about World War II. He's a good guy, but when you get him started on World War II, you might as well pull up a chair because you're going to be there for a while. Anyway, he was talking about **fascism** and **communism** and all of these different kinds of governments I have only heard of in Social Studies class.

It made me realize that I wrongly assumed that all countries are **democracies** like ours. When my great-grandfather was growing up, Germany had a **fascist** government, Russia was part of the Soviet Union and was a **communist** country, **imperialism** was the favorite kind of government for all kinds of kings in the Middle East, and the African countries that weren't run as colonies by France and England were run by **despots.**

My great grandfather lived in crazy times! Today, the Middle East oil countries are still pretty much all run by kings, and Africa is still full of **despots**, but lots of the rest of the countries—like Germany and Japan— have gone **democratic.**

Related Word

nationalism—n. Nationalism is a bad thing when it means you really like your country, but hate all the other countries. Nazi Germany was based on intense nationalism. The Nazis were going to rule the whole world, and kill anyone they thought was unworthy of being a member of the Third Reich.

IDENTIFY THE GOVERNMENT TYPE EXERCISE

Following are some countries that have gone through some big changes over the years. If you don't know what kind of government was in place on the dates I give you (and from the hints in my descriptions), do some research in the library or on the Internet to find out. You will be very surprised by what you find.

Country	Year	Government?
England	1714	King George I assumes the throne.
Texas	1836	Texas is an independent republic.
United States	1897	William McKinley was elected our 25th president.
Germany	1935	Hitler rules with an iron fist.
Jordan	1953	King Hussein assumes his hereditary position.
Cambodia	1976	The totalitarian Khmer Rouge wreak havoc.
England	1979	Margaret Thatcher is elected the first woman prime minister.

Whenever you hear about a country in the news that you don't know anything about, do some research and figure out what kind of government it has. I've been doing this for the last few months whenever I hear about a country in Africa or Asia, because I don't know very much about those two continents. It is really scary how few democracies there are out there!

Exercises

WhizWords

acculturation
colonize
diffuse
genocide
indigenous
inhabitants
migration

Social Studies
Culture Clash

Related Word

**manifest destiny—n.
The United States
used manifest
destiny as its
justification for
destroying the
indigenous cultures
of North America
and committing
genocide against
this continent's
native population.**

A culture is like a situation comedy. It starts out one day with an **indigenous** cast—its original actors. As the **inhabitants** get to know each other, they form relationships, customs and a special language. On a sitcom, the language consists of catch phrases, like "What you talkin bout Willis?" (from *Diff'rent Strokes*) and "yadda yadda yadda" (from *Seinfeld*).

After a few seasons, things usually get a little boring, so a new character or two are introduced to the sitcom's culture. Sometimes they **migrate** from another popular sitcom, hoping that some of their fans from that show will start to watch their new show. The new cast members quickly become **acculturated**, learning the customs and language of their new show.

If the show is popular enough and lasts long enough, some of the cast members may leave and star in their own spin-offs (like *Angel* spinning off from *Buffy the Vampire Slayer*), thereby **colonizing** another night of the network's primetime lineup. As long as the ratings stay high, everyone is happy, and the shows live on. But when the ratings dip for a period of time, there is only one fate for a sitcom culture: **genocide**. The show is killed off.

The actors that do survive usually wander around for a while, getting a few small parts in bad movies and doing some commercials, before they **diffuse** across the sitcom landscape, starring as different characters in different shows, becoming **acculturated** to newer, more powerful sitcoms.

CULTURE CLASH ANALOGY EXERCISE
That was really fun to write. So for this exercise, I want you to use my little story as a model and think of another analogy for how cultures clash, mingle, and mix with one another. I used the rough and tumble world of television sitcoms. Here are a few topics you can use to write a short story about cultures clashing:

Pro sports teams	Neighboring schools
Pop music groups	Neighboring states
Toy companies	Political parties

You don't have to use these suggestions, just make sure you use all of the "Culture Clash" words in your analogy. When you are done, check the words against the definitions and see if you used them correctly.

WhizWords
**abolitionist
bias
discriminate
emancipation
feminism
integration
intolerant
oppress
persecute
segregation
stereotype
suffrage**

Social Studies
Inequality

People rebel because they feel they are being **oppressed** or **discriminated** against. **Feminists** fight for the rights of women every day because women don't have the same rights as men. **Abolitionists** fought for the freedom of slaves, who didn't have any rights at all. In fact, the history of our country is filled with situations where individuals had to overcome **bias**. It was once common to **discriminate** based on race and gender. And our country is called the land of the free! So you can just imagine what life is like in countries where equality isn't even talked about, much less strived for.

Luckily in the United States, we have made great strides. There is pretty much universal **suffrage** now—everyone over the age of 18 can vote. Our public schools, public places, and the military are all **integrated**, too. **Segregation** used to keep white people and black people apart.

Even so, there is still a lot of **intolerance** around. Lots of the advances in equality have happened in the past 20 or 30 years, but old habits die hard. So some people still use **stereotypes** to judge those who are different than they are.

Related Word
diversity—n.
variety.
Diversity and
integration can
help people
learn that
stereotypes
and biases
are shallow
and stupid.

SUFFRAGE FOR FASHION MODELS EXERCISE
The fight for equal rights is a serious business. People have given their lives so that others might have equal opportunity. However, for this exercise, let's lighten things up a little. Pretend there is only one group left in this country that is being discriminated against: skinny fashion models. Now, get a pencil and paper and write a make-believe history about how skinny fashion models go from being segregated, discriminated against, and not having the right to vote to being integrated, having equal rights, and having suffrage in the year 2050. Use as many of the words above as you can.

ESSAY
**The History of Skinny Fashion Models' Fight
For Suffrage in the 21st Century**

WhizWords

ambition
carpetbagger
civic
impeachment
inaugurate
lame duck
mandate
partisan

Social Studies

Politics

The best way to build your vocabulary is to read, read, and read some more. Newspapers are a good source of reading material. You'll find new information about things you're interested in every day.

Did you pay attention to the 2000 presidential race? When it started I didn't pay too much attention. But my dad is such a big Gore fan, he made me go to some rallies, and I started to get excited. And then the election! Nobody won! It took them about a month to figure out who the next president was going to be. It was the first time I stopped thinking about baseball and started thinking about something else outside of school.

The election got me started reading the political stories in the newspaper. That's when I started to realize there were a ton of words I didn't know very well. For example—**carpetbagger.** Have you ever heard that word? And **lame duck.** I mean, what do ducks have to do with politics, especially ducks that waddle with a limp?

Apparently a lot, because **lame duck** and **carpetbagger** kept coming up over and over again, along with **impeachment, mandate,** and **partisan.** It's no wonder they are important to know for the New York State tests. If you know these words, you will be a more informed citizen, and, therefore, probably vote for the right person more often. (At least that's the idea.)

READ THE POLITICS PAGE EXERCISE

Keep this book handy. Pick up the latest copy of your local newspaper. Not the free handout you get at the grocery store with all of the used cars for sale—the real thing. Start with the Sunday paper if you can—it's usually about twice as thick. Now find the stories about local and national politics and start reading. Whenever you see one of the WhizWords above, underline it. Write down the number of times each word appears.

Keep doing this for one week. That's right—read the political stories every day for one week. People may think you are crazy, but do it anyway. You can still read the sports page and the comics (my personal favorites), but read political news first. Underline, count, write the "Politics" words listed above in this chart.

	Day 1	Day 2	Day 3	Day 4	Day 5	Day 6	Day 7
ambition							
carpetbagger							
civic							
impeachment							
inaugurate							
lame duck							
mandate							
partisan							

Which word won? Which came in second? Make sure you know the Top Three like the back of your hand, and make sure you know the rest of 'em like the front of your hand.

WhizWords
boom and bust economy
capital
capitalist
commerce
commodity
economy
entrepreneur
free enterprise
profit

Social Studies

Economics

Did I say this country was all about freedom and equality? Just ask Derek Jeter, who signed a 7-year contract with the New York Yankees for almost $118 million, what this country is all about. Show me the money!

I mean, I love Derek Jeter. He is definitely the best shortstop in the league. But $118 million? I think he gets like $50,000 for each at bat or something like that. I only get $10 a week for my allowance! Maybe Derek can spare a few hundred bucks?

No wonder tests ask so many questions about the U.S. **economy** and our **free enterprise** system. As a citizen of the richest country on the planet, it is important that you know how capitalism works so you can carry on the tradition. Especially if you end up being a major league shortstop.

READ THE BUSINESS PAGE EXERCISE

This exercise is basically a repeat of the politics exercise. After you get done with your week of reading the political stories in the paper, I want you to do a week of reading the business stories in the paper. I know—and you thought it couldn't get any more boring than politics!

Here's your chart for the week:

	Day 1	Day 2	Day 3	Day 4	Day 5	Day 6	Day 7
boom and bust							
capital							
capitalist							
commerce							
commodity							
economy							
entrepreneur							
free enterprise							
profit							

Again, know the Top Three like the back of your hand and the rest like the front of your hand.

Chapter 3

Math

● **absolute value**—*n*. the numerical value of a quantity, regardless of its sign. *Example*: The absolute value of -243 is 243.

● **algorithm**—*n*. a set of rules that specifies how to solve a problem.

● **angle**—*n*. the figure formed when two lines meet at a point. There are three kinds of angles: *acute* (less than 90°), *obtuse* (greater than 90°), and *right* (90°).

acute angle   obtuse angle   right angle

36°

● **angle**—*n*. oh yeah, there are two more kinds of angles—complementary and supplementary. Complementary angles add up to 90°. Supplementary angles add up to 180°.

● **associative**—*adj*. the property that allows two or more real numbers to be added or multiplied, regardless of their grouping, without changing the result. *Example*: Addition and multiplication are both associative.

● **average**—*n*. what you get when you add up a bunch of numbers and then divide by the number of numbers you added up. The average of the numbers 9, 13, 28, 72, 83 = (9 + 13 + 28 + 72 + 83) ÷ 5 = 205 ÷ 5 = 41. So 41 is the average of those five numbers.

● **bisect**—*v*. to divide into two usually equal parts. In math, a line or a point usually bisects another line. It cuts that line in two. Once in science we had to dissect a frog, and I had to bisect its brain—I actually cut its brain in half. I almost fainted.

● **capacity**—*n*. the amount something can hold. *Example*: My dad's Nissan's gas tank has a capacity of 12 gallons of gas.

● **circumference**—*n*. the length of the boundary of a circle. If you took a circle and straightened out the line that surrounds it and measured it, that would be the circumference. The formula to find a circle's circumference is $2\pi r$, with r standing for *radius*.

On the Test

On average, how many plastic bottles are thrown away in New York per day?

WhizList

commission—*n.* a percentage fee that a salesperson gets for making a sale. On tests, sometimes you have to calculate how much in dollars someone makes from a certain percent commission. So if a salesperson gets a 10% commission on a $590 sale, she makes $59.

commutative—*adj.* the property that allows two or more numbers to be added or multiplied in any order without changing the result. *Example*:

$$a + b = b + a \qquad a \times b = b \times a$$

composite—*n.* a number that is able to be factored by numbers other than itself and 1. Just remember that any <u>composite</u> MUST be factorable and prime numbers are NOT <u>composites</u>.

congruent—*adj.* having the same shape and size. If you put one congruent shape on top of the other, they would be exactly the same. In math, this is most often used to describe <u>congruent</u> triangles.

conjecture—*v.* to answer based on incomplete evidence. I would <u>conjecture</u> that you find learning math vocabulary less enjoyable than eating pizza and watching a movie.

consecutive—*adj.* occurring in order, one right after the other. In math, it is most often used to describe <u>consecutive</u> numbers in a number pattern. Players also talk about how hard it is to play on <u>consecutive</u> days in sports like baseball and basketball because they don't get to rest between games.

convert—*v.* to change from one system of measurement to another. Most often used when <u>converting</u> our system of measurements to the metric system. See the conversions page at the end of this section for some common measurements and conversions.

converge—*v.* to come together at a point. Lines <u>converge</u>. So do rivers. In Pennsylvania, the Allegheny and Monongahela rivers <u>converge</u> to form the Ohio River.

coordinate plane—*n.* a plane on which *x* and *y* axes have

WhizTip

To remember composite, think of the word "component." A composite number has "component" factors.

WhizQuiz

Pick the next number in these number patterns:

3, 6, 9, 12, __
–3, –1, 1, 3, __
3/4, 1 1/2, 2 1/4, __

DOUBLE MEANING
convert—v.
To change from one or set of beliefs to another (social studies).

47

Math

$$\frac{3}{5} \leftarrow \textbf{denominator}$$

been added so one can plot coordinates on it.

denominator—*n.* the number under the line in a fraction.

diameter—*n.* the length across the middle of a circle. If you are given the radius of the circle, double it to get the <u>diameter</u>: $d = 2r$.

distributive—*adj.* the distributive property is an algebra property that helps you multiply a single term and two or more terms inside parentheses, when the terms inside the parentheses are like terms. For example:

$$3 (4 +5) = 3(4) + 3(5) = 27$$

divisor—*n.* the number that divides another number (the dividend).

equivalent—*adj.* the same; equal. Sometimes a math problem says "Find the answer that is <u>equivalent</u> to . . . whatever. " All that means is you find the answer that is the same or equal to . . . whatever.

exponent—*n.* a number off to the upper right of another number that shows the power to which the number is raised. That means whatever the <u>exponent</u> is, you multiply a number times itself that many times. For example: $4^3 = 4 \times 4 \times 4 = 64$.

factor—*n.* a number that can be multiplied with others to achieve a product. Hmm. How can I put this? Pick a number. The numbers you multiply to get that number are its <u>factors</u>. Take the number 27, for instance, some of its <u>factors</u> are 3 x 3 x 3 (= 27). Some others are 9 x 3 (= 27). Some others are 27 x 1 (= 27). The number 13 has <u>factors</u> of 13 x 1 (= 13). Note: 13 is also a prime number—which means its only <u>factors</u> are itself and 1.

horizontal—*adj.* straight across. To remember the word, think of a "horizon."

hypotenuse—*n.* the longest side of a right triangle; the side opposite the 90⁰ angle. About the only time you will see questions about the <u>hypotenuse</u> is in questions about right triangles.

integers—*n.* positive whole numbers, negative whole numbers, and zero are <u>integers</u>. No fractions and no decimals are <u>integers</u>—ever! Think of <u>integers</u> as having too much "integrity" to get involved with messy fractions and decimals.

integral—*adj.* in math, it means a number expressable as an integer or a group of integers.

interest—*n.* a charge for a loan, usually expressed as a percentage of that loan. Sometimes a math problem will ask you to figure out how much total <u>interest</u> will be charged over the course of a loan.

intersect—*v.* to cross each other. Lines <u>intersect</u> on graphs. To

remember the word, think of street <u>intersections</u>—where streets cross each other.

inverse—*adj.* in reversed order. The <u>inverse</u> of 2/3 is 3/2.

irrational number—*n.* a number that cannot be expressed as a fraction or decimal. Like π, or $\sqrt{2}$. You can put an <u>irrational number</u> on a number line, but you can't express the number precisely, like you can with 1.5 and –3. (See the definition for *rational number* if it's still confusing.)

justify—*v.* to prove. Most of the time on a math test, it's not good enough to get the right answer. You have to <u>justify</u> your answer by showing how you got to it.

mean—*n.* see the definition for *average*; they are the same thing.

median—*n.* in a group of numbers, it is the one in the middle or the average of the two numbers in the middle. *Example*: Here is a group of numbers: 23, 31, 67, 78, 86, 165, 254. The <u>median</u> is 78—it is the middle number in this series.

mode—*n.* in a group of numbers, it is the number that occurs most often. *Example*: Here is a group of numbers: 23, 24, 24, 25, 26, 27, 28, 29, 29, 30, 31, 32, 32, 32, 33, 34. The <u>mode</u> is 32. It occurs three times—the most of any number in this series.

negative number—*n.* a number less than zero indicated by a minus sign (–). On a number line, the numbers to the left of 0 are <u>negative numbers</u>.

numerator—the number on top of the line in a fraction; the number that is divided by the denominator.

perimeter—*n.* the outside edge of an object or shape. Think about soldiers patrolling the <u>perimeter</u> of their outpost. That means they are patrolling the edges of their camp, making sure the enemy isn't planning any funny business.

perpendicular—*adj.* relating to lines meeting each other at a right (90°) angle. <u>Perpendicular</u> is kind of the opposite of *parallel*. They are mentioned in the same sentence—and the same math problem—all the time.

perspective—*n.* the appearance of depth or three dimensions. Think about drawing a road that recedes into the distance— the sides of the road get closer together as they go away into the distance. Oh heck, sometimes a picture is worth a thousand words, so just look at the picture of the road on the left. That's <u>perspective</u>.

polygon—*n.* a flat shape with three or more straight sides. A <u>polygon</u> is any shape with flat sides, really, from a triangle to a rectangle to an octagon to whatever a shape with 28 sides is

To remember median, **think of the "median" that separates one side of a highway from the other. It runs down the middle of the highway.**

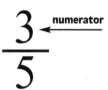

perspective

called, and beyond . . . .

positive number—*n.* a number greater than zero. On a number line, the numbers to the right of 0 are <u>positive numbers</u>.

prime number—*n.* a positive, whole number with only itself and 1 as factors. That means you can't divide any other number into it without getting a remainder. 17 is a <u>prime number</u>. 23 is a <u>prime number</u>. Try all night, you can't divide any other numbers into them without getting a remainder. (See the definition for *factor* for more information.)

On the Test
What is the probability dinner consisted of a hot dog, orange juice, and cake?

probability—*n.* the chance that something will happen. Example: If you flip a coin, the <u>probability</u> that it will turn up heads is 1/2, or 50%, since there are two possible outcomes.

product—*n.* the answer to a multiplication problem. The <u>product</u> of 3 x 6 is 18.

proportion—*n.* a comparison of equivalent ratios. *Example*: 3/6 = 1/2 or 3:6 = 1:2.

On the Test
How would the product **5 x 5 x 5** be expressed in exponential notation?

Pythagorean theorem—*n.* for right triangles, the sum of the squares of a right triangle's sides is equal to the square of the hypotenuse. $a^2 + b^2 = hyp^2$. (See the definitions for *hypotenuse* and *triangles* for more information.)

quadrilateral—*n.* a four-sided polygon. Squares, rectangles, and rhombuses are all <u>quadrilaterals</u>.

radius—*n.* the line from the center of a circle to its outside edge. The <u>radius</u> is half a circle's diameter.

random—*adj.* having no pattern or reason; out of the blue. Lottery numbers are picked at <u>random</u>.

Related Word
random sample—*n.* a group of numbers or values chosen out of the blue.

ratio—*n.* the relationship between two quantities. <u>Ratios</u> are always expressed as fractions though. The <u>ratio</u> of 4 to 9 can be written as 4/9 or 4:9; the <u>ratio</u> of 6 to 7 can be written as 6/7 or 6:7.

rational number—*n.* a number that can be expressed as a ratio of two integers. 7 is a <u>rational number</u> because it can be expressed as 7/1. –2/3 is a <u>rational number</u>. 45.4 is a <u>rational number</u>.

reflection—*n.* a shape that is flipped, so it's the same, but backwards. Think of it like your <u>reflection</u> in the mirror. All the sides are the same length and the angles are the same size; they are just positioned exactly opposite of where they were.

rotation—*n.* movement in a circular motion around a fixed point. When a geometric shape is <u>rotated</u>, its shape stays the same but the side that was on the bottom may now be on the top.

scale—*n.* when talking about models, scale is the relationship between the size of the model and the size of the real-life object. So if a <u>scale</u> model of an airplane is 1:8, that means the real airplane is eight times as big as the model.

scientific notation—*n.* a way of writing numbers in terms of powers of ten. For example, 3,414 is 3.414 x 10³.

subset—*n.* a set within a set.

symmetry—*n.* a balanced arrangement; the stuff on one side of a dividing line matches the stuff on the other. If you draw a line down the middle of your face, the parts on the left match the parts on the right. Your face has <u>symmetry</u>. It is <u>symmetrical</u>. So are some shapes and some graphs.

terminate—*v.* to end; to stop. The word is used in math to describe where decimals <u>terminate</u>. Repeating decimals never <u>terminate</u>—they repeat forever. To remember it, think of the muscle-bound actor Arnold Schwarzenegger. He played the Terminator, and he "ended" any puny little humans who got in his way.

three-dimensional—*adj.* having three dimensions, which gives an object depth. Any real object is <u>three-dimensional</u>. Also written as <u>3-D</u>.

trial and error—*n.* a method of solving a problem with several guesses; your last resort! If you can't solve a math problem the right way, there is always <u>trial and error</u>.

triangle—*n.* shape with three sides and three angles. There are four kinds of <u>triangles</u> you need to know:

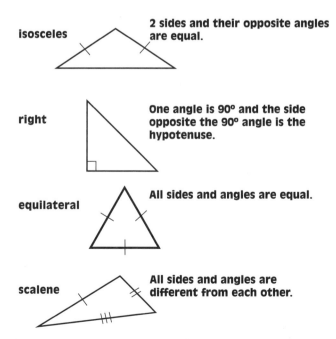

isosceles — **2 sides and their opposite angles are equal.**

right — **One angle is 90° and the side opposite the 90° angle is the hypotenuse.**

equilateral — **All sides and angles are equal.**

scalene — **All sides and angles are different from each other.**

Symmetry

Math

Solve the following problems with the variables *x*=2 and *y*=3

2x
4y
–5y
x – y
2y + 7x
–2x – 4y

variable—*n.* a symbol whose value can change. In math, the <u>variable</u> is usually called *x* or *y*. That means you can plug in different numbers for the variable *x* or *y* or *z* or whatever. To remember the word, think of watching a weather report. The weatherman often says that "winds are <u>variable</u>," and weather itself is always <u>variable</u> (changing).

vertical—*adj.* going straight up and down. Like a flag pole.

whole number—*n.* an integer. Positive or negative. Not a fraction, not a decimal, not an irrational number. Just nice, clean integers are <u>whole numbers</u>.

Math
Measurements Page

METRIC AND
BRITISH IMPERIAL MEASUREMENTS

Measurement conversion charts are provided on most math tests, so it's important you know how to read them. Measuring is the only time I wish I was European. They have things so easy when it comes to measuring. As you probably know, their metric system is all based on tens. Anyway, here are the measurements that are used most often on tests—in metric and British Imperial (that's what we use). Don't ask me why we use British Imperial and the English use metrics. Because I don't know.

BRITISH IMPERIAL
Distance

Foot	12 inches
Yard	3 feet
Mile	1,760 yards

Volume

Pint	16 ounces
Quart	2 pints
Gallon	4 quarts

Weight

Pound	16 ounces
Ton	2,000 pounds

METRIC
Distance

Centimeter	10 millimeters
Meter	100 centimeters
Kilometer	1,000 meters

Volume

Liter	1,000 milliliters

Weight

Gram	1,000 milligrams
Kilogram	1,000 grams
Metric ton	1,000 kilograms

COMMON CONVERSIONS
(ALL CONVERSIONS ARE APPROXIMATE)
Distance

BRITISH IMPERIAL	METRIC
Inch	about 3 centimeters
Yard	about 1 meter
Mile	about 1.6 kilometers

Volume

BRITISH IMPERIAL	METRIC
Ounce	about 29 milliliters
Cup	about 1/4 liter
Gallon	about 3.79 liters

Weight

BRITISH IMPERIAL	METRIC
Ounce	about 29 grams
Pound	about 450 grams
	(about 1/2 kilogram)

WhizWords

divisor
numerator
ratio

Math

Ratios

The great thing about situation comedies is that they are kind of the same every week. The jokes change, the wacky, far-fetched situations change, but the characters and the settings remain the same. Unless, of course, a show decides to take its characters on a whirlwind European vacation to boost ratings during sweeps week.

In fact, you can almost predict how many times a certain character is going to do a certain thing. For example, on the show *Friends*, my sister Hillary and I play this game guessing how many times the character Rachel will touch her hair while she's talking. Last week I guessed 23. I was close—it was 27. Unfortunately, my sister guessed 26, so she won and I had to do the dishes for her the next day.

SITUATION COMEDY RATIOS EXERCISE

For this exercise you need a pencil and paper to keep track of things. You can play this one alone, but it is more fun if you have a friend or relative to compete with. First, pick a TV show. For this example, I'll use the show *Malcolm in the Middle*. Second, pick something to count. My friend Larry and I picked: How many times Malcolm's bullying brother Reese is in a scene, and how many times he hits Malcolm, or anyone else for that matter. Put these in two columns. Third, predict how many times you think each will occur and write that down. Fourth, start counting. Use hash marks to keep track, and when the show is over, tally up your totals.

Reese in scene	Reese smacks someone
(Stan—24)	(Stan—6)
(Larry—19)	(Larry—7)
Actual—23	Actual—3

Compute the ratios for your guesses.

What is the ratio of Reese hits vs. Reese appearances?

Stan	6 : 24
Larry	7 : 19
Actual	3 : 23

Answer additional questions using the data you have amassed. What is the numerator in Stan's ratio? What is the denominator in Larry's ratio? What is Stan's ratio expressed as a fraction?

<u>Extra Credit</u>: Watch the same TV show three times and do this exercise three times. After the three shows, compare the ratios from show to show. How much do they vary?

Circles

So you need more proof that math is all around you? Fine. Let's talk about circles. Circles are obviously everywhere, from the portholes on a ship to the circles under your parents' eyes. The invention of the wheel, the hardest working circle of all time, was a big event, right up there with the invention of Pop Rocks and Napster.

Of course on math tests, you have to do a little more than just appreciate the importance of roundness. You have to be able to calculate **diameters** and **circumferences** of circles of all sizes.

DIFFERENT SIZE CIRCLES EXERCISE

I have given you a variety of circles below. I want you to find the circumference and diameter of each. I'm even going to help you out a bit. Here are the equations for each:

Diameter = 2r

Circumference = 2πr

Note: circles not drawn to scale.

Now, get a ruler. Go and find five more circles in your house and measure the radius—that's half the diameter. Use those measurements to find the diameter and the circumference of the circles you found. Don't know where to start? Try the kitchen, the home of circular housewares.

Note: π is the ratio of the circumference of a circle to its diameter. The actual value for π is approximately 3.14159.

WhizWords

integers
irrational number
negative number
positive number
prime number
rational number
whole number

Math
Number Types

Still not convinced of math's importance in your everyday existence? I was like you once, before I saw the light. One part of math you can't dispute is that numbers are everywhere. We measure ingredients, tell time, and count the days until summer vacation.

What you probably don't do while you are counting the days to summer vacation is think about what kind of number you have in your head. The "31" in "31 days until summer vacation" is an **integer**, a **positive number**, a **prime number**, a **rational number**, and a **whole number**. Those are the kinds of things you need to know for the New York State tests and others. So let's review.

NUMBERS YOU SEE EVERY DAY EXERCISE
Label each of the numbers with all of the number types from above that match. If none match, write "none." I'll do the first couple so you get the idea.

17 years old   integer, positive number, prime number, rational number, whole number

–3 degrees   integer, negative number, rational number, whole number

$.79 Snickers bar _____

.327 batting average _____

2 1/2 weeks _____

4 hours _____

–12 under par _____

a drink coaster with a circumference of 6pi (okay, I'm stretching here) _____

Math
Number Relationships

Whether you believe that math affects your everyday life or not, you still have to take tests about it. One thing that shows up on all sorts of math tests is number relationships. Questions about number relationships usually involve long lists of numbers and ask you to figure out the **mean**, **median**, or **mode**. Sometimes all three.

Just remember:

- mean (means average)
- median (in the middle of the road)
- mode (sounds like most)

So let's get to it.

TEST GRADES EXERCISE

Find the mean, median, and mode of my grades last year on tests in English Language Arts, math, science, and Social Studies.

		Mean	Median	Mode
English	56, 92, 87, 79, 95, 92, 99			
Math	78, 82, 91, 79, 78, 97, 93			
Science	94, 91, 99, 100, 89, 94, 94			
Social Studies	102, 84, 72, 67, 84, 94, 84			

Find the mean, median, and mode of these three baseball players' batting averages over their careers.

		Mean	Median	Mode
Paul O'Neill	.333, .256, .252, .276, .270, .256, .246, .311, .359, .300, .302, .324, .317, .285, .283			
Manny Ramirez	.269, .308, .309, .328, .294, .333, .351			
Alex Rodriguez	.232, .358, .300, .310, .285, .316			
Derek Jeter	.314, .291, .324, .349, .339			
Tony Gwynn	.289, .309, .351, .317, .329, .370, .313, .336, .309, .317, .317, .358, .394, .368, .353, .372, .321, .338, .323			

WhizTip

For more practice, line up your grades from last semester or last year and find the mean, median, and mode.

Chapter 4

Science

absorb—*v.* to soak up. Commercials for paper towels brag about how they <u>absorb</u> spills. You have probably heard your teacher say that she hopes you are <u>absorbing</u> everything she says.

acclimatization—*n.* adaptation to changes in climates. It took a while for the <u>acclimatization</u> of my pet snake to his new aquarium. He didn't eat for a week!

acquire—*v.* to accumulate. An organism is born with certain traits (like big feet) and <u>acquires</u> certain traits (like knowledge and strength).

asteroids—*n.* a bunch of big rocks orbiting the sun, kind of like mini-planets. Most <u>asteroids</u> are in between the planets Mars and Jupiter. In sci-fi movies, space ships are always getting caught up in <u>asteroid</u> belts. Just remember, they are called "belts" because they are "wrapping around" the sun.

atmosphere—*n.* the layer of gases surrounding the Earth or another planet. The Earth's <u>atmosphere</u> is mostly oxygen and nitrogen.

atom—*n.* the smallest unit of an element that has all the properties of that element. Everything in the world is made up of <u>atoms</u>. The <u>atom</u> bomb gets its power from the splitting of <u>atoms</u>—that's how much energy is stored up in this tiny little particle. It's kind of scary when you think about it.

axis—*n.* the center around which something rotates. Axis is usually used when talking about a planet (like the Earth) rotating on its <u>axis</u>.

bacteria—*n.* one-celled organisms. They are all around us, but you can't see them. My mom buys anti-<u>bacterial</u> soap because she thinks me and my sister are getting too many colds—she thinks it's because of all the <u>bacteria</u> on our hands.

beneficial—*adj.* helpful; good. Learning the words in this book should prove to be <u>beneficial</u> to your grades. Hey, it can't hurt!

biosphere—*n.* the part of the Earth and its atmosphere where living things exist.

buoyant—*adj.* it floats! Ivory soap is <u>buoyant</u>, but Zest and Irish Spring sink like stones.

carbohydrate—*n.* a compound composed of carbon, hydrogen,

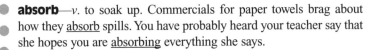

and oxygen. (In foods we eat, most of the <u>carbohydrates</u> are found in sugar and starch.) The night before a baseball game I load up on <u>carbohydrates</u> by eating spaghetti for dinner and two bananas for dessert. For some reason, I never sleep very well.

carnivore—*n*. meat-eater. The most ferocious <u>carnivore</u> known to mice is the house cat.

catalyst—*n*. in science, a substance that speeds up a chemical reaction. Fire is a <u>catalyst</u> for turning water into evaporated water.

catastrophic—*adj*. tragic and awful, causing great pain and suffering. I hope Derek Jeter doesn't suffer a <u>catastrophic</u> injury to his knee. That would ruin the Yankees' season.

celestial—*adj*. related to the stars and the universe. Planets and asteroids and suns and stuff are all called "<u>celestial</u> bodies."

centrifugal force—*n*. moving away from the center. When you swing a bucket of water around in a circle real fast, and the water doesn't fall out, that's <u>centrifugal force</u>!

chain reaction—*n*. a series of events in which one thing leads to another, which leads to another. I saw a <u>chain reaction</u> accident on the highway once when a semi jackknifed, and all of the cars behind it ran into each other.

chemical energy—*n*. energy stored in chemical compounds. <u>Chemical energy</u> is usually released in a chemical reaction, when <u>chemical energy</u> changes into heat, light, or electricity.

chloroplast—*n*. the part of a plant cell that contains the chlorophyll.

circulation—*n*. the movement of blood through the body. (See next definition for more.)

circulatory system—*n*. the organs that move blood around the body, including the heart, veins, arteries, and capillaries. Just think of the pipes and plumbing that circulate water in your house. They are your house's <u>circulatory system</u>.

collision—*n*. the slamming of one thing into another. When there is a <u>collision</u> between an opponent's bat and my best pitch, that is not good.

DOUBLE MEANING
catalyst—n. someone who makes things happen. Usually used in Social Studies when talking about a movement or revolution. The feminist movement's leader, Gloria Steinem, was a catalyst for change for women in the 1960s and 1970s.

Antonym

centripetal force—n. moving toward a center. It's what keeps the planets orbiting around the sun.

complex—*adj.* complicated; not simple. There is almost nothing about science that isn't incredibly <u>complex</u>. The Earth, the universe, your body, the birth of a flea: all of these things are very, very <u>complex</u>.

component—*n.* a part of a system or machine. The <u>components</u> of my stereo are the receiver, the CD player, and the five-speaker surround sound system.

compost—*n.* decayed organic matter that is used as fertilizer. <u>Compost</u> is made of a mixture of dead plants, and maybe manure. It smells awful, but it makes my mom's tomatoes grow fast.

condensation point—*n.* the temperature at which gas condenses into a liquid. Clouds formed over the Yankees' last home game when the air temperature reached the <u>condensation point</u>. Clouds form when liquid collects on dust particles in the air.

conductor—*n.* a material that takes an electric current from one point to another. Copper wire is a good <u>conductor</u>. So are you, so stay away from electricity!

Think of a train conductor getting you from one point to the next.

conservation—*n.* the protection of natural resources. <u>Conservation</u> is important if we are to keep the few natural wonders this country has left, like the Grand Canyon and Yellowstone National Park.

contaminate—*v.* to make impure. Lots of things we do every day <u>contaminate</u> the environment. Driving a car <u>contaminates</u> the environment with carbon monoxide and other gases. Eating fast food <u>contaminates</u> the environment with all of the packaging it comes in, not to mention the pollution from the factories that make the packaging. It's almost like if you don't live in an underground house fueled by solar panels and windmills, you are <u>contaminating</u> the environment! About all we can do is try to reduce the amount of <u>contaminants</u> we produce, but we can never eliminate them.

continental drift—*n.* the theory that the continents are always drifting—they are not fixed. The continents drift only an inch or so each year, but over millions and billions of years, those inches turn into thousands of miles.

continuity—*n.* uninterrupted succession. One of the things that has helped the Yankees dominate baseball for the last five years is the <u>continuity</u> on the team from year to year. There are always some changes, but the best players and the manager have remained the same.

cumulative—*adj.* the adding of things over time. The <u>cumulative</u> effects of age have caused my parents to become forgetful and slow.

DOUBLE MEANING

current—**n. the continuous movement of water (science).**

current—*n.* the flow of electricity.

cyclical—*adj.* happening in cycles. In chemistry, the word <u>cyclical</u> has to do with chemical compounds that have atoms arranged in a closed chain. In real life, lots of things are <u>cyclical</u>. The changing of seasons is the most obvious example.

cytoplasm—*n.* the protoplasm outside the cell's nucleus.

decant—*v.* to pour off the liquid, leaving the sediment behind.

decay—*v.* to rot; to break down. When you die, unless you have yourself cryogenically frozen or you are cremated, your body will decay. I plan on going the cryogenically frozen route, like in the original *Austin Powers* movie. Groovy baby, yeah!

decompose—*v.* to rot; to break down. See *decay* above. Decomposition is a chemical reaction.

dehydrate—*v.* to remove the water from. Dehydrated food like beef jerky has had the water taken out—that's why it's all shriveled. A few games ago I got dehydrated and started feeling dizzy because I didn't drink enough water and it was 98 degrees out.

density—*n.* the mass of an object divided by its volume. Metal is more dense than wood. Hot fudge is more dense than whipped cream.

deplete—*v.* to use up. One of the main problems today is the gradual depletion of Earth's resources.

digestive system—*n.* the parts of your body that work together to break down food so it can be converted into energy. Your digestive system is made up of the alimentary canal, which is basically every part of your body the food touches, from your mouth all the way down to . . . well, you know.

dilate—*v.* to get wide. Your pupils dilate when there isn't much light. That's because when they get wider they let more light in.

dissolve—*v.* to mix with a liquid. Kool Aid dissolves in water to make a tasty, refreshing drink!

distill—*v.* to purify by evaporation and then condensation. Distilled water has had all of the impurities boiled out. What they do is boil the water and then capture the steam—that steam doesn't have any of the impurities that were in the water. They then drop the temperature on the steam and—ta da!—distilled water.

dominant trait—*n.* when paired with a recessive trait, this is the trait that "wins"—the dominant trait beats the recessive trait. So if the dominant trait in a species of butterfly is big wings and the recessive trait is little wings, a butterfly that has one gene for each will have big wings.

dormant—*adj.* sleeping; inactive. Lots of animals, insects, and plants go dormant over the winter, sleeping until spring. When the Yankees' bats go dormant, that means no one is getting any hits, and the team is doomed.

dynamic—*adj.* related to energy and motion. The New York Knicks have been a more dynamic team since they traded Patrick Ewing. There is more motion in the offense, and they run fast breaks better.

eclipse—*v.* to block the light. When the moon eclipses the sun, it's always a big deal. It's all over the news, people are making special eclipse viewers out of paper and cardboard boxes. It's bigger than

WhizTip

Whenever you see a word with "plasm" in it, you know it has something to do with cells.

Science

Groundhog Day! As you have probably heard a million times, never look at an eclipse. It could make you go blind.

ecosystem—*n.* the combination of organisms and the place they live. Our apartment is an ecosystem all by itself, with its people, plants, pets, and other little friends like spiders, roaches, and mice!

efficient—*adj.* not wasting time or energy. I have often found that I study most efficiently when there is no noise. If I turn on the radio or TV, it takes me forever to get anything done.

electron—*n.* a tiny particle in an atom's nucleus that has a negative charge. There are the same number of protons (+) and electrons (–) in an atom's nucleus. Their opposite charges cancel each other out.

element—*n.* a substance that has only one kind of atom. There are 118 elements. My favorite is helium, because it's the element that makes your voice high and squeaky.

endocrine system—*n.* the body's endocrine glands, ductless organs that secrete hormones directly into the blood. The endocrine system includes the thyroid, pituitary, and adrenal glands, plus a bunch more I don't have room to list here. (See "The Body" exercise for all of the organs involved in your endocrine system.)

endothermic—*adj.* absorbing heat. Think of indoors for endothermic reactions. It's a reaction that brings heat "inside."

entropy—*n.* disorder or chaos in a system. So if the Yankees have three injured players, they have entropy on the team—disorder and chaos.

equilibrium—*n.* a condition in which all forces cancel each other out, resulting in balance. Remember it by thinking of the word "equal." Equilibrium happens when opposing forces are equal.

erosion—*n.* the process of being worn away, usually by water or wind. A huge windstorm in Long Island caused a lot of erosion—all the sand on the beaches was basically blown into the Atlantic.

eruption—*n.* the explosion of a volcano. The eruption of Mount Vesuvius in A.D. 79 ended up burying two entire cities in lava and ash. They have only recently started excavating the site.

evaporation—*n.* the process of a liquid turning into a gas. I left a glass of Kool Aid on my bedroom window sill and forgot about it. A few weeks later, all the liquid had evaporated, and all that was left was red, crusty goo. (Also see the definitions for *distill* and *condensation point*.)

excrete—*v.* to eliminate wastes from the body (blood, tissues, and organs).

exothermic—*adj.* releasing heat. An exothermic reaction happens when substances react strongly with each other. For example, if you mix two substances in a test tube and the tube gets hot, that's an exothermic reaction. Heat has been released. (See *endothermic* for more.)

Whiz Quiz

Name five organisms that are part of an ecosystem at or near your home.
1.
2.
3.
4.
5.

Antonym

exothermic—*adj.* releasing heat. Think of an EXIT sign for exothermic reactions.

Whiz Quiz

Do an Internet search and find the most recent volcano eruption in the United States.

extinct—*adj.* no longer in existence. The dodo bird is <u>extinct</u>—there aren't any of them on the planet any more. Dinosaurs are <u>extinct</u>. My mom says real gentlemen are <u>extinct</u>. (I'm not sure what that means.)

extraterrestrial—*adj.* outside the Earth. Lots of people think there are extraterrestrial beings in outer space. I think they're nuts.

fault—*n.* a break in a rock formation. Earthquakes happen along geologic <u>faults</u>, where a rock formation is broken and two big slabs of rock are rubbing against each other.

fertilize—*v.* to make fruitful or productive. When an animal's egg is <u>fertilized</u>, its offspring begins to grow. When crops are fertilized, they usually produce more fruits or vegetables.

food chain—*n.* a line of organisms that eat each other.

Whiz Quiz

Name three more **extinct** animals or species.

1. _____
2. _____
3. _____

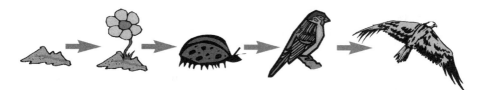

The <u>food chain</u> ends when an animal has no known predator—that means no other animals eat it. (Most hawks have nothing to fear.)

formation—*n.* an arrangement. In geology, a rock <u>formation</u> is an arrangement of rocks with particular characteristics.

fossil fuel—*n.* fuel made from decayed organisms. Coal and oil are actually dead plants and animals that decayed and have been compressed over millions of years into <u>fossil fuels</u>. Wind is not a <u>fossil fuel</u>. Neither is solar energy. They are renewable resources. (See the definition for *renewable* resources.)

friction—*n.* rough rubbing. The <u>friction</u> between two rock formations is what causes earthquakes.

fusion—*n.* in physics, a reaction in which atoms join together. In chemistry, when two substances are melted and mixed together. Basically, <u>fusion</u> takes place when two separate things <u>combine</u> into one thing.

gene—*n.* a section of a chromosome that controls how part of an organism turns out. You have <u>genes</u> that control your eye color, your height, your looks—everything. And we are learning more and more about <u>genes</u> every day. Scientists just completed charting every <u>gene</u> —it was called the Human Genome Project.

generation—*n.* a group of people born around the same time; a stage in a succession. I have heard people calling our <u>generation</u> "Generation I" because we are the first to grow up with computers and the Internet.

genetics—*n.* the study of genes and heredity. The field of <u>genetics</u> is really booming right now. All of the stuff they are finding out about

Whiz Quiz

Think of a name for your **generation** that is better than Generation I.

_____
_____

genes and how they affect our health and everything about us is really cool. Some people even think <u>genetics</u> will be the key to curing cancer!

geology—*n.* the study of rocks and the Earth. If I don't make it as a major league pitcher, I think I'm going to be a <u>geologist</u>. I am almost as interested in earthquakes and volcanoes as I am in sports.

greenhouse effect—*n.* the result of too many pollutants in the atmosphere; they let the sunlight in, but they don't let the heat back out. That causes the atmosphere to act like a greenhouse—keeping the heat in. Some people think the <u>greenhouse effect</u> is causing all the glaciers to melt around the polar icecaps.

groundwater—*n.* the water underneath the soil. Lots of people are afraid things like garbage dumps, strip mines, and nuclear waste sites are polluting the <u>groundwater</u>.

habitat—*n.* the normal environment where an organism lives. A water turtle's natural <u>habitat</u> is a pond. A hermit crab's natural <u>habitat</u> is the ocean. That's why, when we have them as pets, we try to re-create their <u>habitat</u> inside an aquarium with rocks, sand, water, and some driftwood to climb on.

hemisphere—*n.* in earth sciences, the northern or southern half of the Earth. The equator is what separates the northern and southern <u>hemispheres</u>. To remember it, think <u>hemisphere</u> = <u>half-a-sphere</u>.

herbivore—*n.* an animal that eats plants. Cows are <u>herbivores</u>. Horses are <u>herbivores</u>. Vegetarians are <u>herbivores</u>. They all eat veggies, no meats.

hybrid—*n.* the offspring you get when you breed two different kinds of parents. You most often hear the word <u>hybrid</u> when people are talking about plants, like a corn <u>hybrid</u> that fends off insects or a <u>hybrid</u> tomato that is bigger and juicier than any other kind of tomato.

hydroelectric—*adj.* relating to electricity generated by water turning a turbine. My aunt in New York works at a public radio station that is run on <u>hydroelectric</u> power! All their power comes from a dam on a river outside the station.

hydrosphere—*n.* the world's waters. All the oceans, seas, lakes, rivers, streams, and puddles make up the <u>hydrosphere</u>.

hypothesis—*n.* a proposed explanation or statement. Scientific progress is based on proving or disproving a <u>hypothesis</u>. If your <u>hypothesis</u> is "plants are mean," and you do an experiment that proves plants are mean, then your hypothesis is correct. If the experiment does not prove plants are mean, that DOES NOT mean the <u>hypothesis</u> is incorrect, only that your experiment didn't prove it.

igneous rock—*n.* rock that is formed from molten lava. It's not metamorphic, it's not sedimentary—it's igneous!

ignite—*v.* to light on fire. When you <u>ignite</u> your Bunsen burner in science class, it gives off a blue flame.

WhizFact

The United Nations did an environmental study that concluded that the greenhouse effect is going to raise the temperature 2–10 degrees in the next 100 years.

DOUBLE MEANING

hemisphere—n. also stands for one-half of the brain—the left and right hemispheres.

WhizFact

There is a big debate about what to do with the dams in the West that produce hydroelectric power. Some want to destroy them and restore the rivers—and the fish.

Whiz Quiz

Identify the rock's type:

basalt
_____

granite
_____

limestone
_____

marble
_____

immune—*adj.* being resistant to something bad. You often hear this word when people are talking about AIDS. AIDS is an acronym for Acquired Immunodeficiency Syndrome. It's a disease that attacks your <u>immune</u> system, and makes it so you can't fight off any bacteria or other bad germs.

incinerate—*v.* to burn until there is nothing left but ashes. If you flew a space shuttle toward the sun, the sun's heat would <u>incinerate</u> it.

inertia—*n.* resistance to motion. My dad has a lot of <u>inertia</u> on weekends. It's hard to get him off the couch.

inexhaustible—*adj.* never ending. It may seem like the Earth has an <u>inexhaustible</u> supply of oil and coal, but that's not true. If we keep going the way we are going now, we will be out of oil and coal in just a few hundred years. Then what?

infectious—*adj.* capable of causing an infection by microorganisms. Some of the more common <u>infectious</u> diseases include influenza (the flu) and hepatitis.

insulation—*n.* protective material. There are lots of different kinds of <u>insulation</u> in your house. Heat <u>insulation</u> keeps heat from escaping your house. Water pipe <u>insulation</u> keeps the pipes from freezing when it's cold. There is also <u>insulation</u> around electrical wires that keeps the wires from shocking everything they touch!

interact—*v.* to be involved with something else. Science is always testing how different things <u>interact</u>. It can be chemicals that <u>interact</u> with each other in an experiment, it can be animals <u>interacting</u> with each other in a habitat, it can be how the orbits of planets <u>interact</u> with each other.

intestine—*n.* one of two long tubes in your gut where food is digested. The small <u>intestine</u> measures about 22 feet long, and the large <u>intestine</u> measures about five feet long.

ion—*n.* an atom or molecule that used to be electrically neutral, but now it is either positive or negative because it gained or lost electrons. In other words, it used to be neutral (same number of protons and electrons) but it has since gained or lost an electron, so it is a positive <u>ion</u> (lost electrons) or negative <u>ion</u> (gained electrons).

kinetic—*adj.* having to do with movement. Most often, it is used to describe <u>kinetic</u> energy. When a hitter's bat connects with my fastball and sends it out of the park, that, unfortunately, is <u>kinetic</u> energy. To remember <u>kinetic</u>, think of *calisthenics*. They kind of sound the same, and they both have to do with movement.

land subsidence—*n.* the sinking of land. In some arid regions of the Southwest, tapping the water in the water table has resulted in <u>land subsidence</u>. As water is sucked out, the land actually sinks!

lethal—*adj.* causing death. Some states with capital punishment use a <u>lethal</u> injection to kill the prisoners on death row.

light year—*n.* the distance light travels in a vacuum in one year

Whiz Quiz

What's another kind of **insulation**? Try to think of one.

Whiz Quiz

Which is longer?

100 feet of string or your small **intestine**

2,000 miles of highway or your small **intestine**

350-meter running track or your small **intestine**

Six yards of fabric or your small **intestine**

Whiz Quiz

List three things that are **lethal** to humans:

1. _____
2. _____
3. _____

(9.46 x 10^{12} kilometers). It's important to remember that a <u>light year</u> is a measure of distance, not time.

lithosphere—*n.* the Earth's crust. All of the valleys, mountains, plains, and meadows, plus all of the bottoms of the seas, rivers, and lakes, make up the <u>lithosphere</u>.

locomotion—*n.* movement; the act of moving. I feel bad for even saying this, but think of a choo-choo train to remember this word. Sorry.

lunar—*adj.* having to do with the moon. A <u>lunar</u> eclipse is when the Earth blocks the sun's light from the moon. The <u>lunar</u> module is a spaceship that landed on the moon.

mantle—*n.* the layer of rock between the Earth's crust and its core. So, we walk all over the crust, the core is boiling molten rock, and the only thing keeping the molten rock from us crust-dwellers is the <u>mantle</u>. Thank you, <u>mantle</u>!

meiosis—*n.* cell division in sexually reproducing organisms that produces a cell with half the required number of chromosomes that will then link up with the other half of the chromosomes from the other sex partner. Humans have 46 chromosomes—23 from each parent. <u>Meiosis</u> is what produces one of those 23-chromosome sex cells (called gametes).

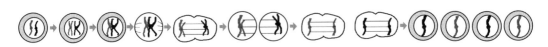

membrane—*n.* as in cell membrane, the outer layer of the cell. The <u>membrane</u> keeps all the stuff inside the cell from floating out AND it keeps out the stuff the cell doesn't need.

metabolism—*n.* the chemical and physical processes that take place in cells; the changes that take place in a body. You have probably heard people say "I have a high <u>metabolism</u>—I eat anything I want all day and I don't gain a pound." Someone with a high <u>metabolism</u> has a body that is working really fast and efficiently to burn up all the food it gets.

Related Word

metamorphosis—n. the change from one thing to another.

metamorphic rock—*n.* rock that was changed from one kind of rock to another by pressure or temperature. It's not sedimentary, it's not igneous—it's <u>metamorphic</u>!

meteor—*n.* the trail behind a meteorite caused by the meteorite entering the Earth's atmosphere. Last year I saw the most awesome <u>meteor</u> shower I have ever seen. It was like the sky was on fire—there were so many <u>meteors</u> burning up as they entered our atmosphere.

Related Word

meteorite—n. a space rock that enters the Earth's atmosphere and makes a meteor.

mineral—*n.* a natural substance with a definite chemical and crystalline composition. A diamond is a <u>mineral</u>. So are gold and silver.

mitochondrion—*n.* the part of the cell that converts food into energy the body can use. It's at the last stage of digestion, working to turn that burger and fries into energy for your body.

mitosis—*n.* the division of a cell into two identical cells; the process of cell division.

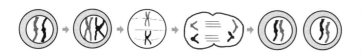

molecule—*n.* the smallest unit of a compound or an element. A molecule of water has two hydrogen and one oxygen atom—H_2O.

molten—*adj.* melted or liquefied by intense heat. The lava that comes out of volcanoes is molten rock.

mutation—*n.* a change in the genes of an organism from one generation to the next. The theory of evolution states that a mutation that helps an organism survive better than others will be passed down from generation to generation, because that organism and its offspring will have a better chance of living and having kids. That's why giraffes have long necks. They lived in a place where the food was up high, so the ones with the genetic mutation that gave them longer necks did better and had more kids than the ones with shorter necks who couldn't get to the food and died.

natural selection—*n.* the theory that organisms best suited for their environment survive and have offspring, and those who are not die and do not have offspring. Also known as "survival of the fittest." Kind of harsh, I know. But it is the way things work in nature. (See *mutation* for more on this.)

neutron—*n.* a particle that's in the nucleus of all atoms (except hydrogen.) A neutron has the same mass as a proton, but no electrical charge (it is neutral). So the nuclei of atoms have protons, electrons, and neutrons (except hydrogen, which has only electrons).

nuclear energy—*n.* the energy released by a nuclear reaction. Nuclear energy makes up a big part of this country's energy production, but not nearly as much as energy produced by burning oil, coal, and natural gas. The thing is, nuclear energy plants can be much more dangerous than other energy sources. If something goes wrong and radiation escapes from a nuclear power plant, people can get sick and die.

nucleus—*n.* 1) in a cell, the center of a cell containing the genes. The nucleus of a cell contains the parts that control the cell, like the nucleus of a baseball team is made up of the players who control whether a team wins or loses. 2) In an atom, the center of the atom containing protons, electrons, and neutrons.

nutrients—*n.* the stuff that nourishes your body. You see the word all the time on vitamin commercials—"VitaMight contains 127

Related Word

magma—n. red-hot rock beneath the Earth's crust.

Whiz Quiz

Name a genetic mutation that helped this species survive:
Giraffe
Human
Elephant
Cheetah

Whiz Fact

Two famous dangerous nuclear accidents:

Three-Mile Island, 1979 Pennsylvania, USA

Chernobyl, 1986 Chernobyl, Ukraine

Science

essential <u>nutrients</u> to keep your body glowing like a lightbulb!" The fact is you get plenty of <u>nutrients</u> from the foods you eat, as long as you eat the right foods.

Related Word

herbivore **and** carnivore **(See the definitions in this chapter.)**

omnivore—*n.* an organism that eats all kinds of food, including plants and animals. Humans are <u>omnivores</u>. So are dogs.

orbit—*n.* the path of one celestial body around another. Planets travel in different <u>orbits</u> around the sun.

organic—*adj.* having to do with living organisms. When you see food labeled "organic" in the grocery store, that means it was grown with all <u>organic</u> materials—no chemicals or man-made substances were used.

organism—*n.* a living plant, animal, bacterium, protist, or fungus. I have used the word <u>organism</u> in tons of these science definitions. It's obviously because lots of science is concerned with the study of <u>organisms</u> and all of the things that affect <u>organisms</u>.

oxidation—*n.* a reaction in which the atoms in an element lose electrons. The most common example of <u>oxidation</u> is the formation of rust. Metal atoms <u>oxidize</u>—they lose electrons—and rust forms.

ozone layer—*n.* a layer of our atmosphere that protects us from harmful sun rays. Pollution is causing holes in the <u>ozone layer</u>, which means those bad sun rays are making it all the way down to the Earth, where they can cause skin cancer. My mom always makes me wear sunscreen when I play baseball because she's worried about the holes in the <u>ozone layer</u>.

periodic table—*n.* the chart that lists all of the elements and their atomic numbers.

5	6	7	8
B	C	N	O
13	14	15	16
Al	Si	P	S
31	32	33	34
Ga	Ge	As	Se

pH—*n.* a measure of how acidic or alkaline a substance is.

photosynthesis—*n.* the process that plants use to turn sunlight into energy. If people could perform <u>photosynthesis</u>, we wouldn't need to eat so much! We could just sit in the sun and get all the energy we need. Instead we have to cover ourselves in sunscreen and stay in the shade. Lucky plants.

physiology—*n.* all of the vital parts and processes of an organism.

porous—*adj.* penetrable by liquid. A sponge is <u>porous</u>. A bowling ball is not <u>porous</u>.

precipitation—*n.* rain, snow, sleet, and hail. The weatherman said the odds of <u>precipitation</u> tomorrow are 50 percent. But he's never right.

predator—*n.* an animal that hunts another. A shark is a fierce predator, hunting other fish continuously, never sleeping, always hungry.

Related Word

predatory—*adj.*
like a hunter.

protein—*n.* a compound in all living things that helps organisms grow and repair themselves. Good sources of protein are beef and beans and eggs—which all happen to be in my favorite omelet!

proton—*n.* a positively charged particle in an atom. (See definitions of *electron* and *neutron*.)

protoplasm—*n.* a jellylike substance that forms all the living matter in plants and animals. That's right, the basis for all living things is a jiggly mass of jelly. Kind of gross when you think about it, so I try not to.

protozoa—*n.* primitive, single-celled organisms. Protozoa might be what the earliest forms of life on Earth were like.

radiation—*n.* the emission of waves or particles. Nuclear radiation is waves and particles given off by radioactive material. It can be really dangerous and even lethal.

recessive trait—*n.* when paired with a dominant trait, it is the trait that "loses."

regulate—*v.* to control. Our brain is our body's main regulator. It controls breathing, heartbeat, appetite—you name it, the brain probably regulates it.

renewable—*adj.* able to be used again. Most often used in the term "renewable resources" to describe sources of energy that can be used again and again. Two examples are wind and sunlight—they are forms of energy that you basically can use over and over, and they never get used up.

reproduction—*n.* the process by which living things produce offspring. Most animals and plants use sexual reproduction, where the offspring gets half its chromosomes from each parent. In asexual reproduction, the offspring gets all its genetic material from one parent. The formation of spores is a good example of asexual reproduction.

resistant—*adj.* able to fight off something. Some crops are engineered to be resistant to certain bugs. Some bacteria become resistant to drugs that are used to kill them. So resistance can be good for us (crops that can fend off pests) and bad for us (diseases that are resistant to treatment).

respiratory system—*n.* the group of organs that keep you breathing. If you think of it in terms of your house, things that circulate air—like fans and air conditioners—are your house's respiratory system. (See the "The Body" exercise for all of the organs involved in your respiratory system.)

satellite—*n.* a man-made object shot into space that orbits the Earth or another planet. Most satellites these days are used for communication, but there are also science satellites and military satellites.

Whiz Fact

The Incredible Hulk was created when scientist Bruce Banner was accidentally exposed to radiation.

Whiz Fact

The first satellite was launched by the Russians in 1957. It was called Sputnik.

scientific method—*n*. the process of observing something, forming a hypothesis for how it works, doing experiments to test that hypothesis, and then drawing conclusions from your results. *Example*: After watching bears at the zoo, you form the hypothesis that bears are dumb as rocks and you do an experiment to test their intelligence. Maybe you ask them their names. When they don't the answer, you conclude your hypothesis is correct—they don't know their names, they must be dumb as rocks. (You can see why the <u>scientific method</u> isn't perfect!)

sedimentary rock—*n*. rock that is formed near the Earth's surface by the accumulation of sediment. It's not metamorphic, it's not igneous—it's <u>sedimentary</u>!

selective breeding—*n*. the process of choosing which plants or animals to breed with each other. You do this when you are looking to promote a particular trait. So if you are breeding poodles and you want poodles with extra long toes, you <u>selectively breed</u> the long-toed poodles. (You give the short-toed poodles away to friends.)

solar—*adj*. having to do with the sun. The <u>solar</u> system is the system of planets revolving around the sun. <u>Solar</u> flares are eruptions that spew from the sun and mess up our television reception. Solarcaine stops sunburn pain when someone you love is hurting.

soluble—*adj*. dissolvable. Sugar is <u>soluble</u> in water. So is Kool Aid.

solvent—*n*. a liquid that dissolves another substance. Water is a <u>solvent</u> for many substances, including sugar, salt, and Kool Aid.

stagnant—*adj*. motionless; not flowing. When water is <u>stagnant</u>, it becomes a prime breeding ground for mosquitoes. When the Yankees' offense is <u>stagnant</u>, that means we need to get some better hitters on the team.

stimulus—*n*. something that causes a response. An organism is always responding to both internal and external <u>stimuli</u>. For example, a toad responds to <u>external stimuli</u> like predators and temperature and <u>internal stimuli</u> like hunger and the urge to reproduce.

sustainable—*adj*. able to maintain over a period of time. One of the ways to fight world hunger is to find <u>sustainable</u> crops that starving countries can grow themselves. There is a Chinese proverb: "Give a man a fish and he will eat for a day. Teach a man to fish and he will eat for the rest of his life." That's the idea behind teaching people in these countries to grow <u>sustainable</u> crops.

synthesis—*n*. the combination of two or more things to make a brand new thing. I think the *Star Wars* movies are the perfect <u>synthesis</u> of special effects and a great story. Combining those two things has made a brand new thing—the best movie series ever.

tectonic plates—*n*. the huge plates that make up the continents and the floors of the oceans. They shift a little all of the time. The friction where the <u>tectonic plates</u> meet causes scary stuff to happen, including earthquakes, mountains, and tidal waves.

Remember, soluble things can be dissolved.

What kinds of sustainable crops do they produce in your part of the state?

temperate—*adj.* not hot, not cold. This word is most often used when talking about temperate climates, where animals and plants thrive because the temperature does not get too hot or cold.

toxic—*adj.* harmful; dangerous. Scientists deal with toxic materials all of the time. Sometimes we even work with them in science class ourselves. Stuff like mercury and dry ice is pretty cool, but they can be very toxic, so be careful.

trait—*n.* a characteristic; a feature. I share a lot of physical traits with my dad—we both have brown eyes, high foreheads, and winning smiles.

transform—*v.* to change from one thing into another. Coal is transformed into diamonds under intense pressure after millions of years.

vacuum—*n.* a space where there is no matter. Lots of science experiments have to be done in a vacuum to work. For example, in a vacuum, a feather and a brick fall at the same rate, because there is no matter—air—to make the feather float more slowly.

vapor—*n.* stuff that looks like mist, fumes, or smoke. Steam is the vapor form of water.

variation—*n.* a slight change. In a science experiment, a variation can affect the result. When I don't feel like going to school, sometimes I try to cause a variation in my temperature by putting a hot towel on my head, then hiding it under the pillow when my mom comes to check on me. It does cause a variation in the temperature of my forehead, but, unfortunately, it doesn't change the temperature on the thermometer. And it makes my pillow wet.

velocity—*n.* speed. The highest velocity I have ever thrown my fastball is 72 miles per hour.

vital—*adj.* necessary to life. Surgeons closely monitor the vital signs of their patients, like blood pressure and heart rate.

watt—*n.* the fleshy orange fold of skin under a turkey's neck. Wait—that's a wattle. A watt is a unit of electricity. If you want to save electricity, make sure all the light bulbs in your house one 40-watt or 60-watt bulbs.

Think of Goldilocks: Not too hot and not too cold, the "temperate porridge" is just right!

Nature is full of transformations. Name three:

1. _____
2. _____
3. _____

To remember vital, think of your favorite TV hospital drama. When they ask for "vital signs," they are asking for the signs of life.

WhizWords

acclimatization
conservation
ecosystem
fossil fuel
greenhouse effect
habitat
organism

Science

The Environment

Related Word

renewable—adj.
Fossil fuels **are**
not renewable.
You use them
once, and they
are history.

Have you ever heard of Woody Guthrie? He was a folk singer who wrote hundreds of songs about America. He would travel the country hitchhiking and riding on freight trains, getting to know the people he met along the way. He ended up writing classics like "This Land Is Your Land," "Pastures of Plenty," and "Do-Re-Mi." (No, not the song about "a female deer" and "a drop of golden sun." A different "Do-Re-Mi.")

Guthrie was also a big environmentalist. He was really alarmed by all of the factories he saw going up around the country. He saw America as an expanse of forests and plains and deserts and lakes and rivers. And he saw it changing into an expanse of roads and cities and houses and, well, people.

My dad loves Woody Guthrie. He is always humming "This Land Is Your Land" and putting in his own words. So when he has to cut the grass he likes to sing, "This land is your land, this land is my land, I've got to cut the grass, that'll keep me smilin'." It can get annoying, but it gave me a great idea on how to remember environment words.

WRITE A FOLK SONG EXERCISE

What I want you to do is use each of these environment words in a verse of "This Land Is Your Land." You want to squish the word and the definition into the verse. It may not win you any Grammys, but if you spend some time on it and fit all six words into six verses, you'll have a little hummable song about the environment. And you can hum it during a test if you need to remember the words!

I'll get you started with a verse about the WhizWord off to the side— **fossil fuel**.

♪ This land is your land,
this land is my land, ♪
Fossil fuel emits carbon monoxide,
when you burn it in your car, man.

If you have another song you want to use instead of "This Land Is Your Land," by all means, go ahead. If you've never even heard "This Land Is Your Land," ask your music teacher to hum a few bars, or go on the Internet to *www.geocities.com/Nashville/3448/thisl1.html* to hear a snippet.

WhizWords
circulatory system
digestive system
endocrine system
respiratory system

Science

The Body

By the end of middle school you should have a pretty good idea of what the different parts of the body do. The four main systems of the body aren't that hard to understand, but there are a lot of organs in each one, so it's good to be able to organize the organs by the systems they are in.

Just remember: the **circulatory system** has to do with circulating the blood. The **digestive system** has to do with organs that help you digest your food. The **respiratory system** does your breathing for you (to remember the word, think about being put on a respirator—a machine that breathes for you). And the **endocrine system**, well, it helps get the bad stuff out of your blood. Crime is bad—so think about the **endocrine system** getting the bad stuff out of your blood. Close enough!

LABELING YOUR INNARDS EXERCISE
I have listed the major organs in each system. Your challenge is to label them in this Britney Spears body outline. Check the answer key when you are done.

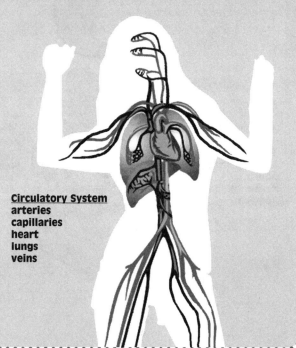

Circulatory System
arteries
capillaries
heart
lungs
veins

Science

Digestive System →
anus
esophagus
large intestine
mouth
small intestine
stomach

Respiratory System →
diaphragm
lungs
nose
pharynx (throat)
ribcage
trachea

The Body

Endocrine System →
adrenal glands
hypothalamus
ovaries (female)
pancreas
pituitary gland
testes (male)
thyroid gland

WhizWords

asteroids
eclipse
extraterrestrial
light year
lunar
meteor
orbit
satellite
solar

Science
The Universe

Related Word

celestial—adj.
Asteroids and
satellites are
both celestial
bodies, as they
are part of the
universe.

Sometimes I just lie on my back in my backyard at night and look up at the sky and imagine what the astronauts on the International Space Station must think when they look out the window. Have you ever seen the movie *Apollo 13* or spent any time on NASA's website? The pictures of space from the windows of spacecraft are just incredible.

And now it looks like normal citizens are going to be able to go into space, just like the astronauts. In 2001, an American businessman named Dennis Tito became the first space tourist when he paid $20 million to join a Russian space crew on a trip to the International Space Station. So someday, you may get to travel in space, whether you're an astronaut or not.

DRAWING THE UNIVERSE EXERCISE

For this exercise you get to draw and label the universe, from the perspective of an astronaut on the old Mir. I have provided the Earth, its moon, and the sun. You can draw and/or label the rest of the "Universe" words above. For example:

LABEL OR DRAW
distance to sun in light years
a partial eclipse
the moon's orbit
a satellite

WhizWords
dominant trait
gene
genetics
recessive trait

Science

Genetics

My friend Gene has curly red hair and freckles just like his father and all of his brothers. That's how I remember that a **gene** is the part of the cell that decides which characteristics will be passed from one generation to the next.

But sometimes **genetics** don't work out quite so logically. For instance, my sister Hillary is really tall: 5'9". Both of my parents are short. So am I. So what happened to Hillary? There must have been a **recessive** "tall" **gene** that both of my parents carried that, against the odds, made it into my sister. The same goes for her eye color. My parents both have brown eyes. I have brown eyes. My sister has blue eyes. So what happened to Hillary? Again, a **recessive trait** in both my parents ended up being expressed in my freaky sister. Here's how that happens:

See *Innerspace!* It's a movie that came out in 1987 about a Navy pilot who gets miniaturized and injected into the body of a hypochondriac.

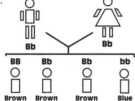

As you can see, the odds are great that my parents would have children with brown eyes, because that is the **dominant** gene for eye color. All you need is one brown eyes gene to have brown eyes. Hillary just got lucky and received a **recessive** "blue eyes" gene from each of my parents.

MOVIE AND TV STAR RECESSIVE TRAITS EXERCISE

Pick out two movie stars. I am going to pick Cher and Billy Crystal. Now, pick a trait. I am going to pick foot size and make big feet dominant and little feet recessive. Draw a chart like the one I drew above, giving each either two dominant genes (FF), two recessives (ff), or one of each (Ff). See how their children would turn out. Here is my Billy + Cher drawing.

I don't even want to think about what the rest of their bodies would look like.

Exercises

WhizWords

continental drift
erosion
fault
geology
mantle
tectonic plates

Science

Geology

WhizTip

Want to learn about New York's geology? Start by going to www.albany.net.

Living in New York, you can forget that the world is a big mass of sliding **tectonic plates** drifting toward and away from each other, causing havoc where they butt up against each other. All of the "mountains" out here are pretty much hills. But anyone who has studied the history of the Earth—and anyone who lives in California—knows that beneath us is a molten core of boiling rock, yearning to break free!

When you think of it this way, **geology** is pretty cool. In addition to studying the process of **continental drift**, geologists get to hunt for wild-looking fossils and try to piece them together like giant jigsaw puzzles. You can see why there are so many geologists running around, predicting earthquakes and digging up dinosaurs.

EARTHQUAKE EXERCISE

Unfortunately, geology is not always fun and games. Every once in a while a big earthquake hits and people lose their homes and sometimes their lives. The same forces that create mountains also create terrible tragedies.

For this exercise, I want you to research a recent earthquake. There was a massive earthquake in India in 2001 that killed tens of thousands. There was also an earthquake in San Francisco in 1989 that ruined the freeway system and caused a World Series game to be postponed (the game was taking place when the earthquake hit).

Once you have compiled some information on an earthquake, turn the page. Write a short essay in the space provided using the words above to explain the tectonic shifts that caused the trembler. Underline the WhizWords in the essay.

Essay

EXPLAIN THE TECTONIC SHIFTS BEHIND A RECENT EARTHQUAKE.

Chapter 5
Test Instructions

Use your pencil when you have reading passages on tests. Underline the topic sentence of each paragraph and circle proper names. It will help slow you down and help you when you refer back to the passage for information.

Circle your answer to the following best questions:
Which word best describes George W. Bush?

man   woman   child

What is your best prediction of how the Yankees will do this year?

better   worse   same

Which word best supports this sentence: "Albany is the capital of New York."

right   maybe   wrong

according to the passage—this phrase means "after reading this passage, this is what you think happened." When you see this phrase, you know the answer to the question is right in the passage you just read. You don't have to use your imagination or remember what you learned in class to find an answer. The answer to the question is in the reading passage.

accurate—*adj.* exactly right. As in "Which of the following is an accurate statement?" This means "Which statement matches the information given?" *Example*: If the information says Hillary spit out her broccoli away when her mom wasn't looking because broccoli makes her sick, an accurate statement would be "Hillary can't stand broccoli," NOT "Hillary can't stand her mother."

approximate—*v.* to come close to; to estimate. Sometimes tests ask you to approximate—that means you are supposed to use the information they give you to make an estimate. Estimates are answers that are close to the real answer. When your car breaks down, the repair shop gives an estimate on how much the repairs will cost. This is approximately how much it will cost. It may be a little more, it may be a little less.

best—*adj.* you'll see this word a lot: "best represents;" "best estimate;" "best prediction;" "best describes;" "the best summary;" "best supported by information in the passage." It means you have to use your "best judgment" and pick the "best answer." You may have a set of answers that all seem like they could be right, and you have to choose the one that is the best (more right than the others).

clues—*n.* something that helps answer a question or solve a problem. As in "Using the information in the passage and the following clues . . . ." Clues are your friends. If a test gives you clues, spend time reading them.

compare and contrast—show the similarities and the differences. Tests love for you to compare and contrast things because it's a great way for them to figure out if you understand what you are reading and writing.

conclude—*v.* to form an opinion based on information. As in "The reader can conclude . . . ." That just means "What did the reader (you!) get from reading this passage?"

conclusion—*n.* an answer reached. As in "What conclusion can be drawn from the graphs shown?" All the question is doing is asking you for an answer.

convince—*v.* to persuade. As in "information to convince the reader . . . ." Some tests ask you if an author provided enough examples to convince you of something. So if I wanted to convince you the New York Yankees are going to win the World Series this year, I'd have to provide reasons to persuade you.

corresponds—*v.* matches; agrees with. Sometimes you are asked to pick the answer that corresponds to the data in the question. That just means it matches. So a test may have a statement like:

The *Star Wars* trilogy became the highest grossing movie series ever, earning more than $1 billion.

And then it says:

Pick the statement that corresponds to the data given in the statement:

> A) The *Star Wars* trilogy lost money.
>
> B) The *Star Wars* trilogy won three Oscars.
>
> C) The *Star Wars* trilogy made a lot of money.

details—*n.* facts or evidence. As in "Use details from the reading passage to answer the following question . . . ." Details are all the little things that come together to create the big picture.

determine—*v.* to figure out. As in "Determine a value for each variable," and "Show the work you used to determine your answer."

equivalent—*adj.* the same as. Test questions—especially math and science test questions—often want you to find things that are equivalent to one another. That just means finding an answer that is the same as something in the question. So if a test wants you to find the equivalent to a dozen eggs, you pick 12 eggs. If a test wants you to find the equivalent of 1/2 meter, you pick 50 centimeters.

expression—*n.* a way of saying something, usually with an

Related Word
The word corresponds is related to the words accurate, equivalent, and exactly.

81

Test Instructions

equation. As in "which <u>expression</u> could be used . . ." or "which <u>expression</u> represents . . . ." So you are trying to match the <u>expression</u> to the passage. A passage may say:

Tim bought five eggs, dropped three, and then purchased five more. Which <u>expression</u> represents Tim's egg-buying experience?

A) 5 + 3 + 5

B) 5 − 3 − 5

C) 5 − 3 + 5

fact—*n.* something that actually happened or actually exists. As in "Which of these is a <u>fact</u> in this passage?" Note: When there is a question about a <u>fact</u>, there is often a question about opinion, too. (See the definition of *opinion* for more.)

main idea—as in "the <u>main idea</u> of the story." You get a <u>main idea</u> by reading a passage carefully. Sometimes the title of a reading passage offers a clue about the main idea. Sometimes it's better to decide the passage's main idea *before* you read the answer choices. You will usually find your main idea among the answer choices. But if you read the answer choices first, it can get confusing, because usually all the ideas in the answer choices are in the passage, but they aren't the <u>main idea</u>.

main purpose—the writer's motivation for writing, as in "The author's <u>main purpose</u> in this passage is to…" In "main purpose" questions, you are looking for what the author was trying to accomplish with his writing. Sometimes his <u>main purpose</u> is to scare you (horror novel). Sometimes his <u>main purpose</u> is to convince you to believe something (persuasive article). Think about how you felt after reading the passage. Informed? Amused? Inspired? How you felt is probably the writer's <u>main purpose</u>.

most likely—as in "Which is <u>most likely</u> to be true . . . ." This means the answer is what is probably going to happen. At least there is a better chance it will happen than the other answers. The answer to a "most likely" question usually isn't spelled out in the reading passage. You have to guess what is <u>most likely</u> to happen based on the information in the passage.

mostly about—as in "This article is <u>mostly about</u> . . . ." This is just like *main idea*.

opinion—*n.* something someone believes or thinks, whether it is true or not. As in "Which is an opinion in this passage?"

probably—*adv.* most likely. Most often used as "<u>probably</u> felt . . ." or "<u>probably</u> believes . . ." or "<u>probably</u> thought . . . ." It just means that the passage doesn't actually state what a character or writer believes, but from reading it, you should be able to tell anyway.

reasonable—*adj.* logical; showing good judgment. <u>Reasonable</u> is like "best." *Examples*: "Which is a <u>reasonable</u> total cost . . ." and

Circle the facts, underline the opinions.

The Yankees hit 205 home runs in 2000.

They are going to win the World Series again.

The Yankees beat the Rangers when they met in the playoffs in 1998.

Derek Jeter is the best shortstop ever.

Think of the main idea as the "main tent" at a circus. That's where the main show with the elephants and the trapeze artists is. The other parts of the circus are in smaller tents. They are all part of the circus, but the main tent is the main idea. So when you look at the answer choices, think "Is this the elephant in the main tent, or the bearded lady in a smaller tent?"

"What is a <u>reasonable</u> prediction . . ." and "What is a <u>reasonable</u> conclusion . . ." and "What is a <u>reasonable</u> length . . . ." Who is the most <u>reasonable</u> person you know? The most <u>reasonable</u> person I can think of is the newsman Tom Brokaw. You know who I'm talking about—he reads the nightly news for one of the networks. He seems very <u>reasonable</u>—like I can trust him. Whenever I get a question asking "what is a <u>reasonable</u> . . . whatever," I think— which answer would Mr. <u>Reasonable</u>, Tom Brokaw, choose? You can do the same thing. Just pick out the most <u>reasonable</u> person you know and try to choose the answer you think he would choose.

reason to believe—as in "gives the reader <u>reason to believe</u>…" This means the passage makes you think one way, not the other way. For example, here's a sample passage: "The New York Giants have drafted the 10 best players in college football, and the other teams in the NFL weren't allowed to draft anyone at all." This passage gives you <u>reason to believe</u> that:

  a) The Giants will get better.

  b) The other teams in the NFL will get better.

The answer is (a). You have <u>reason to believe</u> that if the Giants got all the good players and the other teams didn't get any players at all, the Giants will get better, not the other teams, even though it doesn't actually say that in the passage.

rounded to the nearest—as in ". . . <u>rounded to the nearest</u> thousand." When a test question asks you to round off, that means you go to the place given (tens, hundreds, thousands) and round up or down. If the next number is 5 or higher, you round up 1. If the next number is 4 or lower, you round down 1. On these questions, it is very important to pay attention to whether the question is asking you to round to tens, hundreds, thousands, or whatever.

suggests—*v.* leads you to believe. As in "The information in the passage <u>suggests</u> . . . ." This just means the information doesn't come right out and say something, it just hints at it. It's kind of like a "probably" question—you have to read the passage carefully and trust your understanding of it.

support—*v.* to provide evidence for. As in "Use details from the article to <u>support</u> your answer." This means you can't just state your opinion or give an answer. Not only do you have to give the right answer, you have to show how you got it.

true—*adj.* correct. As in "Which value for *q* will make the statement true?" As they say at the end of that "Whassup!" commercial: True.

WhizTip
Trust your instincts on these probably questions. If you probably think a writer probably meant to say the Earth is flat, and that is an answer choice, you are probably right.

On the Test
What value for *b* will make the following statement true?

Test Instructions

Reading Carefully

Related Word

**conclude—v.
to form an
opinion based
on information.
Tests are always
asking you
what you can
conclude from a
reading passage.**

As you know by now, being able to read things and understand what you read is very important when it comes to doing well on tests. The way tests figure out how well you are understanding things is by using these three "Reading Carefully" phrases. So it helps if you get used to answering questions that use these words, not matter what kind of reading it is.

My favorite things to read are, in order, the online *New York Times* sports page, *Sports Illustrated*, and the Harry Potter series. So as long as J. K. Rowling keeps pumping out books, the Yankees keep playing baseball and the *New York Times* keeps going strong, I am going to be reading for the rest of my life. You probably have some favorite reading materials, too. That's what we are going to use in this next exercise.

READING WHAT YOU LIKE EXERCISE
Open your favorite book, magazine, or newspaper, or go to your favorite website. Pick a passage or article that's about one to three pages long. If you use a website, print out the article. Read it carefully, using your pencil to circle important names and underline important sentences. Take your time, really "get into" the writing. When you are done reading, write three sentences that start with these words:

> The author's purpose in this article is . . . .
> According to this passage, the author thinks . . . .
> The main idea of this passage is . . . .

Do this with at least five different kinds of writing. If you like doing it, do it a lot. It takes, like, five extra minutes, and you'll end up remembering a ton more stuff about things you actually like.

Test Instructions

Probably

Not everything in life is absolutely, positively 100 percent obviously true. Come to think of it, almost nothing is. That means you have to get used to recognizing degrees of possibility.

For example, the New York Yankees are **probably** going to be really good for a long time because they have the best shortstop in baseball, Derek Jeter. And it's **reasonable** to **suggest** that Britney Spears is going to be popular for a long time because she's so . . . talented.

What's my point? My point is that even if you don't know something is absolutely, positively 100 percent obviously true, you can still **probably** know a whole bunch of things. And on tests, one of the keys to doing well is being able to figure out what is **reasonable**, and what is not.

If you are having trouble on tests figuring out what is **probably** true, a good way to get some perspective on things is to think "What would Mr. Reasonable do?" And everyone knows who the most reasonable people on the planet are. Newscasters!

[Related] Word

approximate—v. to come close to; to estimate. Math tests often ask you to approximate something, which means using the information they give you to get an answer in a general range.

MR. REASONABLE EXERCISE

If you don't watch the nightly news already, take half an hour out of your busy schedule for a few nights and watch the Big Three: CBS (Dan Rather), NBC (Tom Brokaw), and ABC (Peter Jennings). Pick the newscaster who strikes you as the most reasonable of the bunch—the guy who would probably pick the right answer. Mine is Tom Brokaw. He seems like he would make a good, reasonable guess.

Now get a pencil and paper. Write your guy's name on the top of a piece of paper. Now sit down with a parent or friend and watch the news! Have your news buddy write down four questions about news stories from the nightly news, using the four "Probably" words. For example:

Is it reasonable to suggest that Iraqi President Saddam Hussein will make nice with President George W. Bush?

Before you answer, think "How would Tom Brokaw answer?" Do this every night for a week, and you'll probably get the hang of the "Probably" words and questions.

Hint: One way to be sure you've come up with the right answer to a question using a "Probably" word is to write a response that includes the word "because," *because* this will require you to go back to the reading passage to find information to prove your point. If you can't find evidence to back up your answer, you're probably wrong.

Chapter 6
All-Purpose Words

List the three classmates you collaborate with the most:

_____

_____

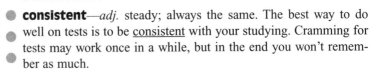

inconvenient—adj. causing a lot of trouble.

collaborate—_v._ to work together. You learn best when you col-laborate in the classroom. My science teacher has us collaborate on projects, but I've been having trouble getting anyone to work with me since I accidentally lit my lab partner's notebook on fire with a Bunsen burner.

consistent—_adj._ steady; always the same. The best way to do well on tests is to be consistent with your studying. Cramming for tests may work once in a while, but in the end you won't remember as much.

constructive—_adj._ helpful. The word is most commonly used in the phrase "constructive criticism," which means you are doing something wrong, but the person telling you is only trying to help by pointing out your errors and showing you how to improve.

contradiction—_n._ something that disagrees with something else. You have probably heard the phrase "a contradiction in terms." That's when two words in a row contradict each other, like: "an easy test." Tests aren't usually easy. Tests also often ask you to find contradictions in stories and passages. That is where two things do not agree with each other.

convenient—_adj._ easy; handy. This book is incredibly conven-ient to keep around. It's small, and it has all the words you need to know. Just put it in your bookbag and keep it there. Whenever you have a question about a word, this book will be conveniently in your bag and you can look it up.

conventional—_adj._ normal; accepted. One phrase that's used a lot is "conventional wisdom," as in: Conventional wisdom says that short people aren't that good at basketball.

logical—_adj._ reasonable; making sense. Logical is kind of the opposite of _emotional._ When you get emotional on tests, you can really mess up. Try to stay logical as much as you can, going from one question to the next without getting too worked up.

objective—_adj._ fair; impartial. To remember this word, just think about what kind of opinions an "object" like a chair would have. Answer: no opinions, _objects_ don't have opinions.

precise—*adj.* exact; accurate. Tests kind of go back and forth from asking you to be <u>precise</u> with your answers to asking you to estimate (make a reasonable guess). So make sure you pay attention to <u>precisely</u> what the text question asks for.

predict—*v.* to guess in advance. Some test questions ask you to <u>predict</u> what will happen in an experiment or in a story. That means you are supposed to look at the facts and make a logical conclusion as to what will happen. (See definitions of *logical* in this section and *conclusion* in English Language Arts.)

relevant—*adj.* related to the matter at hand. Sometimes on tests, you are asked to use only <u>relevant</u> information—that means information that matters (as opposed to stuff that does not matter). For example, if you are taking a test on making cheese, milk is <u>relevant</u>, because it's an ingredient in cheese, while information on fingernails is not <u>relevant</u> (it is <u>irrelevant</u>).

strategic—*adj.* planned. This word is used a lot when talking about war—especially about generals' "<u>strategic</u> maneuvers." Chess is a game that also requires a lot of "<u>strategic</u> maneuvers." Speaking of which, when you are taking tests, it can be important for you to have a <u>strategy</u> going in, like "I am going to stay cool no matter what" or "I am going to do the easy questions first and the hard ones second." Both of those are good <u>strategies</u>.

systematic—*adj.* acting according to a plan or system. <u>Systematic</u> is a lot like *strategic*—they both are used a lot when talking about a powerful person, like a general or dictator, who has a master plan and a *strategy* or a <u>system</u> to carry it out.

tangible—*adj.* touchable; real. This book is <u>tangible</u>—it is real and you can touch it. The word is used a lot in the phrase "<u>tangible</u> benefits," which means good things that actually happen. For example, my friend Larry realized the <u>tangible</u> benefits from all his time in the kitchen when he won first prize in the cake baking contest.

Try to predict your grade on a test before you take it, then see how close you are to your prediction.

Antonym

irrelevant—adj. not pertaining to the matter at hand.

intangible—adj. not touchable.

WhizWords
All of 'em.

All-Purpose Words
Celebrity Hot Tub

You can also do this with flash cards—write the word on one side, and the question using the word's definition on the other.

Did you ever want to be one of those reporters on *Entertainment Tonight* or *Extra* or *Access Hollywood* who just spends all her time running around, interviewing celebrities at parties? Or better yet, a VJ on MTV who just hangs out and chats with bands and singers who come by the show's studios? Well, I have.

My idea is that I'd have the celebrities over to my house and interview them sitting in my parents' hot tub. We'd relax in our swim suits, sip lemonade, and talk about whatever they wanted to talk about. I'm actually thinking about doing this for my public access cable station or doing a webcast. I just haven't figured out how to arrange the microphones without all of us getting electrocuted.

CELEBRITY HOT TUB EXERCISE
For this exercise you are going to need a pad and pencil. Write down "Celebrity Hot Tub" at the top of a page. Now, go to one of the chapters and write down ten words that you are having trouble with. Just read through the words and definitions from one chapter and pick out ten words where you are still a little shaky. Here are ten I picked from Social Studies:

compensation	pragmatist
deter	provoke
dominate	resolute
impose	subversive
insurgent	utopia

Now form a question that you would ask a celebrity who joined you for Celebrity Hot Tub. Use the definition as part of your question. For example, this is a question that I would ask supermodel/actress James King.

Q: Ms. King, are you a pragmatist about your acting career? By that, I mean, are you realistic about the roles you are going to get?

After you have written questions using ten words from one chapter, go ahead and write questions with words from the other chapters, too. Keep these all in one place so you can go back and review them (or ask them, should you ever find James King sharing your hot tub).

All-Purpose Words
Word of the Day

You know those daily calendars that look like a block of Post-it Notes? You peel off a page every day and learn something new—every day. My favorite one is the *Far Side* cartoon-a-day calendar. I even have a bunch of my favorite *Far Side* calendar pages taped to the inside of my locker. My favorite one is "The Night of the Crash Test Dummies"—it has all these crash test dummies attacking some poor guy in his car.

Anyway, the cool thing about that calendar and others like it is that you get to see something new every day. And that's the best way to learn vocabulary words, by using them every day.

Related Word

consecutive—adj. occurring in order, one right after the other. For this exercise, you are going to be learning words consecutively, one right after the other.

VOCABULARY CALENDAR EXERCISE

Until I can convince my book's publisher to make a WordWhiz word-a-day calendar, you are going to have to make one for yourself! This exercise will take an afternoon, so wait until you have a few hours to kill—maybe when it's raining out or you are home sick from school—to get started.

You can make this calendar one of two ways:

> With a brick of Post-It Notes
> With some other "something-a-day" calendar

If you use Post-its, first go through them and make them into a calendar, writing down the days and months left in this year. (Use a wall calendar as a guide.)

If you use another calendar, find one that has a lot of empty space where you can write down a word and its definition.

Now, there are over 600 words in this book. You need to choose the 365 words (or however many days are left on your calendar) that you need to learn the most. Now write the word and its definition on your calendar.

When you are done, put your calendar somewhere where you will see it the first thing in the morning: by your bed, on the sink in the bathroom—wherever. Read the word-of-the day aloud, repeat it and its definition three times, then put it in your pocket. Try to use that word as much as you can on its day.

Word Whiz

New York Middle School

Answer Pages

Here are my answers to the Whiz Quizzes and Exercises.
To find out how you did on quizzes and exercises that ask you
to write essays, create calendars, and otherwise use
your creativity, run your answer past an adult who can decide whether or not
you have used the vocabulary words correctly.

English Language Arts

Whiz Quizzes
page 8
Use an adjective or adverb to describe each of these words:

I go to a *small* school.

My mom had a *fabulous* shopping experience last week—she got four pairs of shoes for the price of one.

Difficult tests make me concentrate even harder.

My soccer team has *bright* green uniforms.

I play a lot of *physical* sports, like soccer and football.

The pizza at lunch today was *unbelievably* chewy. It was like eating pizza-flavored gum.

Use the analogy of a staircase to describe how your grades have been going recently:

My grades started low and have been climbing a steep staircase. Now they are nearing the top.

page 11
List three euphemisms you or your parents use:

If I don't get *Tomb Raider* I'm going to lose it.

Grandpa Hattan is a few cards short of a full deck.

If the Yankees lose again I'm going to be ill.

page 12
Identify the part of speech of the following words:

blonde—adj., n.
threaten—v.
fake—adj., n., v.
mambo—n., v.

Note: As you probably can tell by now, many words have meanings that have multiple parts of speech.

page 13
Write the following sentences using metaphors:

Pam is <u>greased lightning</u>.

James is <u>two French fries short of a Happy Meal.</u>

Fabio <u>vacuums up ice cream</u> like there is no tomorrow.

page 14
Write down the premise of the last movie you saw:

There's Something About Mary
Everyone was in love with a girl named Mary, but only one geeky guy was her soulmate.

page 15
Write a one-sentence summary of the last book you read:

The Old Man and the Sea
An old man hadn't caught any fish in quite some time, then he caught the biggest fish anyone had ever seen and had to bring it in to shore all by himself.

Social Studies

Whiz Quizzes
page 29
List three things you once thought were futile:

Getting Latrell Sprewell to play for the Knicks.

Reaching a height of 5 feet tall.

Achieving the high score on *Arctic Thunder*.

Who was the first president to be impeached?

President Andrew Johnson

page 34
Name your nemesis!

The big bopper on our team's arch rivals the Buford Bears. I don't know his name, but he keeps hitting home runs off of me.

Name your favorite team's main opposition:

The Boston Red Sox

page 37
List three regulations at your school:

1. No chewing gum in class.
2. For boys, no T-shirts: all shirts must have collars.
3. For girls, no skirts: only dresses and slacks.

page 39
Name a limitation you have had to transcend in your life:

I was really impatient a few years ago and got upset over unimportant things. I have worked hard to be more patient and mellow.

Exercises
page 41
Government

Country	Year	Government
England	1714	Monarchy
Texas	1836	Republic
United States	1897	Democracy
Germany	1935	Fascism
Jordan	1953	Monarchy
Cambodia	1976	Despotism
England	1979	Democracy

Answer Pages

Math

Whiz Quizzes

page 47
Pick the next number in these number patterns:

3, 6, 9, 12, <u>15</u>
–3, –1, 1, 3, <u>5</u>
3/4, 1 1/2, 2 1/4, <u>3</u>

page 48
Circle the integers.
1/2
.6
(6)
(−6)
(−2)
(0)
3.2
6.9
3/4
(17)
(−12)
(243)

page 52
Solve the following problems with the variables $x=2$ and $y=3$:

$2x = 2(2) = 4$
$4y = 4(3) = 12$
$-5y = -5(3) = -15$
$x - y = 2 - 3 = -1$
$2y + 7x = 2(3) + 7(2) = 6 + 14 = 20$
$-2x - 4y = -2(2) - 4(3) = -4 - 12 = -16$

Exercises

page 54
Ratios and Proportions

What is the numerator in Stan's ratio? 6

What is the denominator in Larry's ratio? 19

What is Stan's ratio expressed as a fraction? 6/24 = 1/4.

page 55
Circles

Quarter	d= 2(1 in) = 2 in	
	c= 2π(1 in) = 2π in	
CD	d= 2(7 cm) = 14 cm	
	c= 2π(7 cm) = 14π cm	
Tire	d= 2(12 in) = 24 in	
	c= 2π(12 in) = 24π in	

Number Types
page 56
$.79
positive number, rational number

.327
positive number, rational number

2 1/2
positive number, rational number

4
integer, positive number, rational number, whole number

-12
integer, negative number, rational number, whole number

6π
irrational number, positive number

Number Relationships
page 57

	Mean	Median	Mode
English	85.71	92	92
Math	85.43	82	78
Science	94.43	94	94
Social Studies	83.86	84	84
O'Neill	.291	.285	.256
Ramirez	.313	.309	none
Rodriguez	.300	.305	none
Jeter	.323	.324	none
Gwynn	.336	.329	.317

Science

Whiz Quizzes

page 62

Name five organisms that are part of an ecosystem at or near your home.

1. roaches
2. cat
3. mice
4. tomato plants
5. ants

page 63

Name three more extinct animals or species.

1. Dodo bird
2. Tasmanian tiger wolf
3. Sea cow

Think of a name for your generation that is better than Generation I.

Generation Perfect

page 64

Identify the rock's type:

Basalt—igneous
Granite—igneous
Limestone—sedimentary
Marble—metamorphic

page 65

What's another kind of insulation?

My sleeping bag insulates me from the cold when I camp out.

Which is longer?

100 feet of string
2,000 miles of highway
350-meter running track
Your small intestine

List three things that are lethal to humans:

1. Some kinds of cancer
2. Power lines
3. Extreme hot or cold

page 67

Name a genetic mutation that has helped this species survive:

Giraffe—long neck
Human—opposable thumbs
Elephant—big tusks
Cheetah— extreme speed

page 70

What kinds of sustainable crops are produced in your part of the state?

In New York City, none.
But upstate, they grow apples.

page 71

Nature is full of transformations. Name three:

1. Caterpillars transform into butterflies.
2. Ice transforms into water (and vice versa).
3. Seeds transform into flowers.

Answer Pages

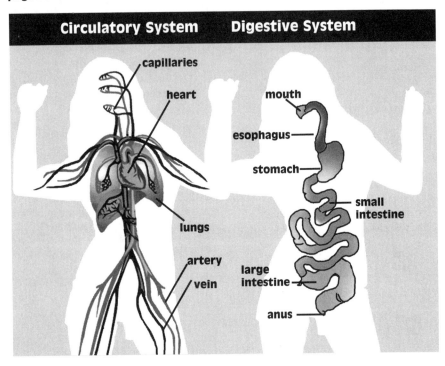

Circulatory System

capillaries
heart
lungs
artery
vein

Digestive System

mouth
esophagus
stomach
small intestine
large intestine
anus

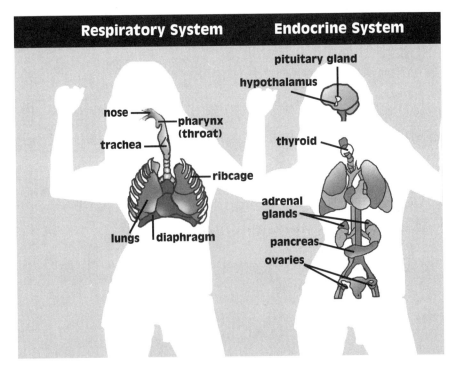

Respiratory System

nose
pharynx (throat)
trachea
ribcage
lungs
diaphragm

Endocrine System

pituitary gland
hypothalamus
thyroid
adrenal glands
pancreas
ovaries

Test Instructions

Whiz Quizzes

page 80

Circle your answers to the following "best" questions:

Man
Better
Right

page 82

Circle the facts and underline the opinions.

The Yankees hit 205 home runs in 2000.

They are going to win the World Series again.

The Yankees beat the Rangers when they met in the playoffs in 1998.

Derek Jeter is the best shortstop ever.

All-Purpose Words

Whiz Quizzes

page 86

List the three classmates you collaborate with most:

Frank
Judy
Mookie

Also Available